NEVER TELL ANYBODY ANYTHING

YOU CAN GET THEM TO DISCOVER FOR THEMSELVES

JAMES E. TAULMAN

BROADMAN PRESS
Nashville, Tennessee

© Copyright 1990 ● Broadman Press
All rights reserved
4234-33

ISBN: 0-8054-3433-X
Dewey Decimal Classification: 268.6
Subject Heading: TEACHING
Library of Congress Catalog Card Number:
Printed in the United States of America

Unless otherwise indicated, Scripture quotations are from the King James Version of the Bible. Scripture quotations marked (GNB) are from the *Good News Bible*, the Bible in Today's English Version. Old Testament: Copyright © American Bible Society 1976; New Testament: Copyright © American Bible Society 1966, 1971, 1976. Used by permission.

Library of Congress Cataloging-in-Publication Data

Taulman, James E., 1937-
      Never tell anybody anything you can get them to   discover for themselves / James E. Taulman.
             p.   cm.
      ISBN 0-8054-3433-X
      1. Christian education--Teaching methods. I. Title.
   BV1534.T38 1990
   268'.6--dc20   89-37251
                                                                                  CIP

Introduction

Teaching the Bible can be fun. If the Bible is the greatest Book in the world, then our teaching methods should reflect that greatness.

Each week thousands of teachers meet Sunday School or Bible study classes. These teachers use many different teaching methods—some of which are not the best to use in teaching the Bible. These methods range all the way from "read this verse and tell us what it means" to a formal lecture in which no one but the lecturer ever speaks.

In spite of the poor methods that teachers use, people are learning about the Bible and how to apply it to their lives. However, the time invested in Bible study can pay greater dividends. I have committed my life to providing material for teachers to use and to showing teachers how exciting teaching God's Word can be. Teachers who use good teaching methods can help their class members discover more of God's truths than they are now discovering.

The teaching suggestions in this book will help teachers of the Bible communicate the eternal message of the Bible in a manner that will make people want to learn. Sunday School does not have to be dull and boring. It can be exciting.

Sunday School teachers represent a tremendous untapped force for good. They represent a potential for a real breakthrough in reaching people for Christ and instructing those people in the Scriptures. This book can help

teachers achieve that breakthrough. It will help people
want to learn what God says in His Word. It will create
excitement in Bible study. It will improve the quality of
teaching and the quality of learning that takes place in
any classroom.

Let me share a couple of ways you can use this book.
The primary purpose is to stimulate your thinking and to
show you how to create and use all the teaching methods
mentioned in this book.

A second way the book will help is by providing resources for you. Check the Scripture index to see if I have
dealt with a particular verse. You might find a biblical
simulation, a biblical skit, or some other help that you
could use in a lesson you are teaching.

I am grateful to my colleagues at the Baptist Sunday
School Board in Nashville. They have shared with me
many ideas and allowed me to pick their brains about
teaching methods. I am particularly grateful to Larry
Shotwell who took the time to read the manuscript. My
prayer for you is that this book will help the Bible come
alive for you and those you teach.

Contents

1
The Fun and Benefits
of Discovering for Yourself

The young man was obviously in love. Love was written all over his face. His palms were sweaty. He had a funny feeling in his stomach. He was starry-eyed. He went to his father to talk to him about what it meant to be in love. His father rose to the occasion and said, "Son, being in love is great. You'll want to hold her hand and kiss her. Take me to her, and I'll show you how to kiss her, then I'll tell you all about it!"

You're not quite sure that's the way it happened? Well, maybe it didn't happen quite like that. If you don't believe that example, try this one.

The hostess had invited several guests to dinner. When they entered the dining room, they saw a beautifully decorated table. A white-linen tablecloth covered the table. Fresh-cut flowers formed the centerpiece. Blue candles resting in silver holders provided the light. However, only one place setting appeared at the long dining table. When all the guests were seated, the hostess explained: "I have discovered the most delicious new dish—Shrimp Rothschild. It is absolutely scrumptious. I want to tell you how it tastes." So she began to take bite after bite of the succulent dish in front of her guests and gave them a thorough description of the delicate flavors of the dish.

What? You don't believe that either? Let me try one more.

A Sunday School teacher invited a whole classroom of

people to study the Bible. She told them that she had discovered the most marvelous truths from God's Word, and
she wanted to share those truths with them. She began to
describe in minute detail the delights of the Scriptures
without ever letting class members ask questions or participate in any way. She told and told and told.

Did I finally find an example you believed? What
makes the difference? In the first two examples, the father
would be considered foolish, and the hostess would be
considered rude. Far too often the teacher in the third example would be considered brilliant!

However, the same principles apply to good Bible
teaching as apply to most other areas of life: never tell
anybody anything you can get them to discover for
themselves.

Notice how those who try to sell us something use this
principle. Car dealers give test drives—even offering special incentives at times to get people to discover the advantages of their particular car. Food distributors give
away free samples to get us to discover how great their
product tastes. Real estate developers give free weekends
at their resorts to get people to discover the luxury for
themselves. "Try it for 30 days" is the theme of many a
sales pitch. Salespeople know that once you have discovered the benefits of their product, you are much more
likely to keep it.

Then, the same people who have been bombarded all
week by this "discover for yourself" approach come to
church on Sunday or attend a Bible study during the
week. They are asked to sit silently and let someone do all
the discovering for them. Are they enthralled? Excited?
Satisfied?

Of course not! Why should they be excited when all
week everybody else who has been trying to sell them
something has been trying to get them to *discover* the thrill
of using their product? Is it any wonder that many

people—especially adults and youth—do not like to go to Sunday School? The real miracle is that many do go. That is a testimony to the power of God's Word. But if that Word has such a powerfulness under that kind of teaching, think what it would accomplish if teachers would help others discover God's truths for themselves instead of just telling them.

This book will challenge you to *want* to help people discover the great truths in God's Word. It will also give you some ideas about how you can do that. Leading people to discover the truths in God's Word is fun and rewarding. I hope you will be convinced that discovery learning is not only fun but also more successful than simply *telling* people what you want them to know.

A good rule to remember in teaching adults the truths of the Bible is the following:

> Tell me, I forget.
> Show me, I remember.
> Involve me, I understand.[1]

Results of Leading People to Discover for Themselves

Leading people to discover things for themselves is fun. I enjoy cooking. Recently, I baked a cranberry brownie layered with strawberry ice cream, interspersed with cranberry sauce and pecans, iced with whipped cream, and decorated with chocolate hearts. It was a joy to watch people bite into the desert and hear them ooh and aah.

That was almost as much fun as sitting with a small group of people and being able to see someone studying a certain Bible passage suddenly stop, look up, and say: "I never knew that!" Leading people to discover the truths in God's Word is exciting.

It is also rewarding. Leading people to discover more about God and themselves keeps me going. It makes my day. It makes me feel like I have done something good and worthwhile. I recently received a letter from a Sunday School teacher who had used some of the material I had worked with. An eighty-six-year-old man accepted Christ at the conclusion of the lesson. That is *real* discovery learning! Sunday School teachers can have no greater thrill than having a person discover the Savior's love and grace. That's what discovery learning is all about.

However, leading people to discover God's truth for themselves is time consuming. This kind of teaching "can come forth by nothing, but by prayer and fasting" (Mark 9:29)—to paraphrase the Scriptures. Leading people to discover Bible truths for themselves will take some time to learn. Usually, we will need to learn a whole new approach to teaching than we have been using and have seen others using.

Nearly everything we know about sharing God's truths goes against this kind of teaching. Young preachers go to college to learn to be preachers. The professors *tell* them—and often poorly—great truths. The preachers graduate and go to seminary. They are exposed to even more telling. When they graduate, they begin to teach and preach—usually by telling. The teachers they teach in their churches learn to *tell* people the truths instead of leading them to discover those truths for themselves. So the cycle continues to repeat itself. However, the sequence can be broken. It can change.

Change can happen at any time. A teacher who has been telling can experience the thrill of seeing others discover God's truths for themselves.

Possibly a word of warning needs to be given. Not everybody will take to discovery learning when first exposed to it. Some do not want to learn anything. They attend Sunday School classes because a spouse or parent brought them (or some other less-than-admirable reason), and they are not about to open their lives to God's Word.

Others have gotten so accustomed to sitting in a class room and having the teacher do all the talking, that they do not want anyone to upset that routine. After all, they have been able to sit and let their minds wander while the teacher does all the telling.

Elray Allen shared with me a conversation she had. A woman who had been sitting in a class where the teacher did all the telling got a new teacher one Sunday. The member came out complaining that she did not like the new teacher because the teacher made the members do her Bible study for her. Elray replied: "Do you realize what you have said? You have said that you have not been doing any Bible study yourself!"

Leading people to discover for themselves requires a great amount of Bible study. Somehow the idea has gotten abroad that only those teachers who tell are the real scholars. Don't you believe it! A teacher who only tells, knows (or at least uses) only one method of teaching. However, teachers who lead a class to discover must use a multitude of teaching methods. Not only must they know the Scriptures, they must know many ways to present the Scriptures, so their class members can discover what the Scriptures mean. Teachers who are serious about leading people to discover God's truth will know the Bible inside and out—as well as knowing good teaching methods.

Discovery teaching has another plus in its favor. You may not know all there is to know about a subject. However, if you are good at leading your class to discover for themselves, they may discover something that you did not know. Had you only told, they would not have learned that information at that point in their lives.

Discovery learning works especially well in studying the Bible. The Holy Spirit works in the midst of those studying the Bible and can lead any person to a new insight or understanding. If you only tell and never give an opportunity for interaction with your members, you are

cutting yourself off from insights the Spirit has for you
and your class.

Are you with me? I hope you have caught the idea by
now. What I have tried to get you to discover (I started to
write *tell you!*) is that it is more enjoyable for the people
you teach to discover God's great biblical truths than for
you to tell them those truths. However, there is another
point. Not only is discovering Bible truths for yourself
more enjoyable, but people just learn better if you lead
them to discover ideas instead of telling them the ideas.
When we study something as important as God's Word,
people must learn its great truths. Let's look at some of the
ways people learn.

How on Earth Can I Learn Anything?

Theories! I'm really not too concerned about your being
able to cite a lot of theories. There are many theories
about how people learn. They are important, but for our
purposes we need to discover on our own some ways people learn. If I'm going to do what I'm asking you to do, I'm
not going to be able to tell you a bunch of theories. I'm
going to have to get you to discover for yourself how
adults learn. That approach makes it much more exciting
for me—and I hope more valuable for you, too.

Think back to a time when you learned something.
Think about the event and the circumstances:

What did you learn?
What was the setting?
How did you learn it?
What made you want to learn it?
What good did it do you to learn it?

Let me share with you when I learned not to throw
green apricots at pretty girls in swings after dark. I was
about eight years old when I learned this seldom-known
fact. In our backyard were several apricot trees. In the

spring of the year, the trees produced abundantly. Tennyson had said it a long time before I was eight, but there was an older girl who lived next door who was about sixteen, and in the spring of the year my thoughts had turned to love. Oh, I would never have admitted it then, but I can remember the feeling over forty years later.

One evening right after it had gotten dark, this beautiful girl was swinging in a swing. Because I was in love with her (don't ask me to explain what I am about to say), some other boys and I picked up the green apricots that had fallen from the trees. Then, from the cover of trees and darkness, we threw the green apricots at her. Unknown to us, one of our missiles hit her in the eye.

When my father came to talk to me about what had happened, I learned a lesson: never throw green apricots at pretty girls in swings after dark. (And I never have again, to this day! Honest!)

Now, let's analyze this experience. What did I learn? I learned a lesson that helped me get along in life. The lesson probably kept me from experiencing severe corporal punishment. I know it kept me from being frustrated. We moved shortly after that, and never again have I had apricots to throw! If I had continued my desire to throw apricots, I would be extremely frustrated today. More important, I learned that people must act in certain ways in order to live in this world and get along with other people.

The setting was in the backyard of our home and later in my bedroom when my father confronted me. Learning can take place anywhere. However, the setting can be important, depending on what you want people to discover. I could never have learned not to throw green apricots if I had not had green apricots to throw.

How did I learn this lesson? I learned it because I hurt somebody I loved. True, my father's explanation helped, but it was not nearly as important as having inflicted hurt.

What made me want to learn not to throw green apricots at pretty girls in swings after dark? Several factors motivated me: love and fear were at least two factors that motivated me.

What good did it do me to learn this lesson? It helped me learn that I had to respect the rights of others in order to get along in life. It also taught me to express my feelings in more direct ways. (But that's a different story!)

Let's see how many things we have discovered about learning in this experience. For us to learn, we must be involved in the experience. We learn few things in abstract. When we are involved, learning will take place much easier and will stand a much better chance of affecting the way we live.

The experience I shared with you happened to me, but my sharing it with you can help you learn the same lessons that I learned—provided I am able to share it with you in such a way that you become involved in the experience. I'll have more to say about this later when we talk about case studies.

Learning can take place anywhere. It does not have to be inside an educational institution. However, certain features have to be present. We have to be exposed to a teacher and to a teachable event. In this case, my father became my teacher. I also taught myself some things.

I wanted to learn because I was motivated—both by love and fear. My motivation was quite intense.

Learning this lesson the first time I had the opportunity made my life a whole lot easier. I eliminated a lot of stress on my part by not having to repeat the experience.

If discovering ideas for yourself is more fun, and if people learn better by doing that, why do we not engage in discovery learning more often? Let's discover some ways we can help those in our classes discover the exciting truths of God's Word.

Teachers can use a lot of ideas to help members discover

truth for themselves. All these ideas or methods of teaching have their place. However, teachers of teachers have agreed that certain teaching methods are basic. These basic ideas include lecture, group discussion, questions and answers, case studies, and brainstorming. Let's look at each of these teaching methods to discover ways we can use them to help class members discover the truths of the Bible for themselves. Then we'll consider some other methods that will be even more helpful in getting your members involved in learning God's Word.

Let me offer one other word in this connection. Whatever method you use, don't use the same method all the time. Gaines Dobbins is credited with saying that the worst teaching method is the one used all the time. Class members get tired of the same teaching method just like I would even get tired of eating ice cream all the time—well, maybe not ice cream! So, regardless of the methods you use in teaching, vary them regularly.

2
How to Say Something and Have People Remember It

Lecture is the most popular method of teaching. It can be an effective method. It can also be the most boring of all methods. Someone has defined a lecturer as someone who talks in somebody else's sleep![1] Although lecture is the most popular method, it is also the most difficult to use.

It isn't difficult (at least for most people who are teachers) to say something. Most teachers can find enough in the Sunday School quarterlies or Bible teaching materials they use to fill up thirty to forty-five minutes of time—especially if they let the group talk about Saturday's ball game or the party the night before.

However, presenting a good lecture is a difficult task. By good I mean a lecture that enables people to discover God's truth for themselves. If it doesn't do that, as far as I am concerned, it is not a good lecture. However, you can use a lecture that enables people to participate in discovery learning. Let's discover some ways we can use lecture and still get people to discover some things for themselves.

Lecture has its place in helping people learn. A lot of great teachers have used lecture. For an example of a good lecture and Lecturer, read Matthew 5—7. When only the teacher has certain information, when time is limited, or when the group is too large to use other methods of teaching, lecture should be used.

Lecture can help your class members gain biblical knowledge or understand certain great truths. However, it does not help them learn to apply those truths to their lives. In this sense, lecture has limitations.

You may be thinking that you would be satisfied if your class could even gain biblical knowledge or understand great truths. That would be an improvement in many Sunday School classes or Bible study groups. Good Bible teaching can do even more than that. Good Bible teaching can help members analyze and evaluate problems and help them change their attitudes and their behavior. Good Bible teaching can make an eternal difference.

Lecture itself is not wrong. This book is a type of written lecture. I am trying to convince you to help your class members discover truth for themselves. However, I am not using just one method to convince you. Rather, I am using a variety of teaching methods.

What makes lecture less than desirable is that many teachers use lecture all the time. They never use any other method to enhance the discovery quotient. When used properly, lecture is a significant tool to help Sunday School teachers lead the members in their classes to discover God's truth.

If all that is true, then let's discover some ways to say something and have people remember it. One other word: all that follows is based on the belief that you have made adequate study of the text you are lecturing on. Using the best teaching methods will not make up for sloppy study and scholarship. You should be the best scholar you can be. Then take these suggestions and use them to present the fruits of your study. Think back to the last lecture you heard. This may have been at a seminar, in a Sunday School class, in a worship service, or in a classroom. Was it a good lecture? Was it interesting? Did you learn anything from it? Do you remember anything the lecturer said?

Let's assume that you answered yes to all the above questions. (Congratulations! You are much more fortunate than most people who have heard a lecture recently.) Let's analyze why you could answer yes. How many of the following did the speaker use?

> Interesting illustrations
> Change in voice inflections
> Understandable language
> Visual aids
> Study guides
> Pretest—Posttest
> Listening teams
> Wrote on chalkboard or paper
> Asked you to take notes
> Changed position when appropriate
> Shared personal experiences
> Spoke to life's needs

If you answered yes to all the questions in the earlier paragraph, the speaker probably used several of these teaching methods in the lecture. If so, I would suggest that you try to hear this speaker as often as possible, so you can observe the methods he or she uses. You can discover good teaching methods for yourself in that way.

Why would these methods make a lecture more interesting?

Few people wake up on Sunday morning thinking, "I wonder what message Nahum has for me today?" (At least I never have, but then, people tell me I am different!) However, people do wake up every morning of the week wondering if God will punish people who cheat others and defy God. If you are seeking to teach a lesson on some difficult book or passage of the Bible, you must use interesting illustrations that touch people's lives. Whether the illustrations are relevant to your members' lives will determine if the illustrations are interesting and memorable.

To begin a lecture with an *interesting illustration* that

touches people's lives will grab their attention and give you an opportunity to lead them into Bible study. I tried to do that with the opening illustrations in the first chapter. You will have to determine if I succeeded in capturing your attention. Once you have captured your class members' attention, then you can lead them to discover the basis of your statements in God's Word. Leading your members into Bible study is the real purpose. To grab their attention and then not offer them the solid meat of the Word is like having someone promise you a thousand dollars only to find out they didn't mean it. You must lead your members into the real meat of the Scriptures. You should base what you have to say on God's Word. That makes it important. God's Word alone is eternal. People come to listen to you because you speak for God. They will come to your class not because of your authority, power, and creativity, but because you base what you have to say on God's Word.

You can make a lecture more interesting by *varying the inflection* and tone of your voice. While this is not a teaching method, it is important in discussing lecture. This sounds so elemental, but many speakers maintain the same pitch and volume throughout. Using dramatic pauses can create interest and get people's attention.

Let me give you a short test. Which is more interesting?

APPROACH 1: To have the speaker begin by saying, "Today we are going to study the exciting Book of Nahum. Please open your Bibles to Nahum 1."

APPROACH 2: To have the speaker lean forward a little, pause until everybody is looking at her, and then say just loud enough so people can hear: "Have you ever wondered why the wicked get away with their evil and the good people suffer?"

APPROACH 3: To have the speaker say, "Well, I guess

we better get started. The lesson isn't too interesting to-day, so I'll get through it as soon as possible, and then we can talk about something that is interesting."

In the first approach, the speaker has *told* me that the Book of Nahum is exciting. I don't want her to tell me; I want her to *show* me that it is interesting.

In the third approach, the teacher has already told me that I have wasted my time by coming this morning. So I can tune her out and start thinking about my plans for the afternoon, or where we're going for dinner after church.

The second approach would catch my attention. I would be interested in hearing what a teacher had to say about that question based on God's Word. I often wonder why evil people prosper, and good people suffer and die.

Use *understandable language* in a lecture. Don't talk about the transubstantiationary implications of the eucharistic feast in Pauline epistolary usage. Instead, talk about how Paul referred to the Lord's Supper in his letters.

Visual aids can also help you teach so people will remember. Back to Nahum. The book is about Assyria. How many people in your class know where Assyria was? Do they know the difference between Assyria and Syria? A good set of maps will help you explain the location of the country in relation to Judah. The map will also help you focus the attention of your class members and get them all doing the same thing at the same time (looking at a map).

You can use other forms of visual aids to enhance your lecture. If you have access to an overhead projector, you can use overhead cels. You can use a clear cel and a marker instead of writing on a chalkboard or sheet of paper. However, I find that using an overhead projector is too much of a problem for a weekly Sunday School class or Bible study group. If you want to use one, great! It does add interest. However, I make poster strips and put them on the wall as I discuss certain points. You can use posters of all types to capture the interest of your listeners. Using these visuals will help you retrieve your listeners if their attention has wandered.

Give a *test* when you finish your lecture. Tell the class in advance that you are going to give them a test at the conclusion of the lecture. Ask them to take notes on your lecture. A variation of this would be to give a pretest at the beginning of the class and then give the same test at the end of the class period to see if they learned anything. The members would know exactly what to look for. If you give a test be sure you include in your lecture all the points on the test.

Listening teams can also help people remember what you say. Divide the class into two or three groups. (Groups can be as small as one person.) They don't even have to move their chairs to form a group. Ask each group to listen for a particular idea and report on their assignment at the end of the lecture. If they know they are responsible for some particular bit of information, they will pay closer attention.

A *study guide* or listening guide can also help people remember what you say. Prepare your lecture. Then pick out the main points you want to make and construct a study guide in which you ask the class to listen for those facts. (1) You can write these questions on the chalkboard or on a large sheet of paper and post them where all the class can see them. (2) You can write them on an overhead cel. (3) You can make up a guide for each group. (4) You can make up an individual listening guide for each person.

Writing on a chalkboard, a large sheet of paper, or overhead cel will also help people remember what you say. As you lecture, write the main points of your outline on a large sheet of poster paper. For each point use a different color felt-tip pen. This little bit of color will help even more than using one color all the way through.

Using *personal experiences* will help the class remember what you are trying to communicate. Let the class know how you feel. A Sunday School class is not an appropriate place for baring all the gory details of a sordid past. However, it is a place to share that you have some struggles and difficulties in your life. We relate much better to weakness than we do to strength. Most members of Sunday School classes imagine that teachers never have any of the difficulties they have. When they discover that teachers are also human, they will be able to relate much better to what you have to say.

Change your position occasionally. Above all, don't stand behind a large lectern. The lectern sets up a barrier that will keep you from being accessible to your class. It will also set you up as an authority. Many teachers complain that their class will not discuss anything. One good way to encourage discussion is for the teacher to sit down. Sitting in a circle or sitting around a table will place you on equal footing with the rest of your members. Get up and move to the chalkboard, locate a city on a map, or point to some other visual aid. This movement will help focus member's attention on you if their minds have wandered.

Ask your members to take notes. As you lecture, ask your members to look for certain points and write them down. You can give them pieces of paper, or they can write the notes in the margins of their quarterlies. Occasionally, you may want them to remember an important point. Ask them to write the point down. People remember ideas better if they write them than if they just hear them.

Even if you do all these things, you must *speak to life needs*. You can entertain and make your lecture interesting. However, if your lecture doesn't speak to the life needs of your members, they will not learn. If they have not learned, you have not taught. You have only entertained —or wasted your time and theirs. You can be assured that you will speak to life needs if you will stay true to the Bible. The Bible deals with life. If you teach it, the Holy Spirit will communicate to those you are teaching.

Although you may not have been able to observe it as you did some of the other features, your good lecturer also had an aim in mind. He knew where he was going. He had a goal he wanted to accomplish. If you want to accomplish a task, you must know what the task is.

I have a friend who is an accountant. One year following the tax season, he and his wife went to the airport with their bags. They walked up to the ticket counter and asked for two tickets on the next flight. They had no idea where they were going until they got the tickets.

This might work for a distraught tax consultant. However, it does not work for a teacher of the Bible. You must know where you are going. Not many classes will be as indulgent as my friend's wife was in going with him wherever he went.

How Can Lecture Help in Discovery Learning?

Can you use lecture to help people discover God's truth? Most certainly! Lecture—and by lecture I am assuming a well-presented lecture which uses many of the methods we have discussed above—can share information that people do not have. A good lecture can also whet people's appetite for more information. It can also inspire people to action and decisions for Christ.

Now I would like to ask you to do some discovering of your own. Look back over this chapter on lecturing. Look for the things that you would like for the next lecturer you hear to use. Pick those methods that you think would make the lecture most interesting.

What did you discover? My guess is that you listed a lot of other teaching methods and ideas rather than straight lecture. Lecture by itself is not too high on the list of effective methods to use to help people discover God's truth for themselves.

However, it does allow you to use a lot of other methods that can be combined with it. That is the strongest

point that can be made in lecture's favor from the view-
point of discovery learning.

I would not suggest that you never use lecture. I use it
in some form every Sunday morning in my Sunday
School class. However, I would suggest that if you want
to use discovery teaching, do not rely on lecture as your
primary method. You have many other options that will
accomplish the purpose much better. They are more interesting, too.

3
Does Anybody
Have Any Questions?

I read of a speaker at a high school commencement service. Everything that could go wrong did. Murphy's law was proven again and again. Babies cried. He encountered all kinds of distractions. In the midst of the confusion, he noticed an elderly gentleman sitting in rapt attention who appeared to be hanging on to every word he was saying. With renewed vigor, the speaker centered his attention on that one individual and finished his address.

When the service was over, the speaker asked the principal if he would introduce him to the gentleman. "Well, yes, I'll try to introduce you," the superintendent said, "but it may be difficult. You see, the old fellow is stone deaf."[1]

What a letdown, you say? Yes, but have you ever finished a Sunday School lesson and asked a person who had sat looking quite attentive throughout the lesson what the lesson was about only to discover that the person had not heard a word you had said?

One way you can find out if your class members are (a) listening, (b) interested, or (c) understanding what you are saying is to ask questions. Consider the following two situations.

Bill Davis had been teaching a men's Bible class for years. Bill studied hard all week long. He read several different commentaries each week. He was prepared to tell his class more than he possibly had time to tell them each

week. He would sometimes finish his lesson a minute or
two before class was over. When he did, he would ask,
"Does anybody have any questions?"

Sue Johnson taught a coed class of singles. She began
her preparation on Sunday afternoon for the next week.
All week long she thought about the lesson and studied
different commentaries. Often she would begin her class
by saying something like: "I want to share with you an
experience from the life of Jesus. Would you all listen to
discover how this experience of Jesus can speak to the life
of a single today?" After she had shared the experience of
Jesus, she asked, "Sandi, how do you think this experience out of Jesus' life applies to you?"

Which teacher do you think got more discussion from
the class? Which class do you think learned more? Which
class would you rather be in?

Why Use Questions?

Using questions can help you be a better teacher. Questions can also help those in your class discover God's
truths for themselves. Questions can be a valuable teaching method for teachers who try to get their members to
discover truth for themselves instead of just telling them.
Let's look at some reasons that you should use questions.

Questions come in two basic forms: open-ended and
closed. Open-ended questions cannot be answered with a
specific answer. Open-ended questions often begin with
such words as who, what, when, where, why, and how.
Examples: Why did Jesus tell His disciples to pray? What
steps can Christians take to improve their prayer life?
When in your life have you found prayer to be the most
helpful? How do you go about setting up a prayer time?

The second kind of question is the closed question.
Closed questions can be answered with specific answers.

Is the Gospel of John in the Old Testament or New Testament? How many books make up the Old Testament? What was the capital city of Judah?

As a general rule, the open-end questions will serve your purposes better as a teacher. You are more interested in teaching your members how to live rather than only teaching them Bible facts.

However, at times you will want to use questions that call for specific answers. What verse tells us that Jesus died for our sins? Who, according to verse 20, ministered to Jesus?

I have already referred to one reason you should ask questions. Questions allow you to find out if the group heard what you said. You said it, but did the class pay any attention to what you said?

Do you remember Sue Johnson's method of asking questions? She asked the whole group to listen for a particular answer. Then she asked one person to respond. The class did not know which person she was going to call on for the answer. They all had to listen instead of thinking about where they were going for lunch after church. If she had singled out Sandi before she shared the information, other class members could have gone fishing mentally. However, the way Sue did it gained her their attention all the way through. Asking questions can help determine if the class has heard what you said. Knowing you are going to ask questions can help the members stay alert.

You can also ask questions to see if the class has comprehended what you said. They may have heard it, but did they understand it? I remember a woman who was a member of my seminary church. Lucille was an "active" listener. If she did not understand what I said, she would frown visibly. When I saw her frown, I knew I needed to stop and repeat what I had said in a different manner. Questions can help you accomplish the same objective even better. If you ask a question, and the members cannot answer it, or they answer it incorrectly, you can back up and explain what you said in a way the class can understand.

You can use questions to create interest in what you are teaching. If a teacher began a lesson by asking, "Under what circumstances should we obey Jesus' teaching about cutting off our right hand if it offends us?" do you think the class would be interested? I should think so. However, if you use such questions, be sure you can deliver an adequate and appropriate answer. It is unfair to ask such questions and then not give a biblical answer. You may get their attention once, but you lose your credibility if you do not deliver what you promised. The next time you raise such a question, your members will remember when you did not deliver the answer and will tune you out. The supermarket tabloids do this with their sensational headlines. They often promise more in the headlines than they can deliver in the accompanying article. Don't make the same mistake they do.

You can ask questions to involve people in the lesson. If people are drifting away, you can ask them a question and get them involved in the lesson.

Questions can also show the group that you value their input. However, the questions must be genuine. They must not be so obvious that they do not cause any thought. A teacher of four- and five-year-olds asked, "Boys and girls, who created the world?" A five-year-old who had been in Sunday School since cradle roll days replied with real disgust in his voice, "G-o-d, God." Most adults would not be quite as abrupt, but they may be thinking the same thing. They would just be a little more polite.

Questions can also help you determine what the group already knows. If every member of the class can already give you the names of all Judah's kings and the dates they ruled, along with their mothers' names, you probably would not want to spend much time on teaching them those biblical facts. However, if you asked who was king of Judah when the Babylonians captured it and the group answers that it was David, you know you need to spend some time in helping them understand a little bit about the history of Judah.

Using questions can provide answers about biblical facts. Be certain you do not insult the intelligence of the class members by asking questions that are too simple. Be equally careful not to ask questions that intimidate them because the questions are too difficult.

You can also use questions to involve a member who feels estranged or who finds it difficult to participate in the group. However, you might want to consider using the questions in a little different way than you would normally use them. Instead of asking the questions yourself, let the person you are trying to involve ask the questions. Write the question or questions on slips of paper along with the answers. Before class ask that person to raise the questions at the point in the lesson where you want to use the information.

When Should You Use Questions?

I recently received a birthday card from a dear friend who knows how much I love ice cream. (I've never eaten any bad ice cream; some I just liked a lot better than others!) The card read: "Happy birthday to someone who shares my philosophy of life . . . Ice Cream . . . it's not just for dessert anymore."

I look at questions in much the same way I look at ice cream; questions are appropriate to use in teaching at anytime or anyplace. You can serve questions for appetizers, the main course, or desert. You can begin a lesson by asking a question to create interest in the topic. You can ask questions all the way through the lesson. As you guide

Bible study you can check the comprehension level of the group, find out if the group is with you, discover if the group heard what you said, regain a group that has gone to sleep, discover factual answers, and find the position of the group on certain points. Finally, you can ask questions to apply the Bible to the lives of your members.

In each of these situations you can vary the way you use the questions. Let me give just one example. You can raise a question at the beginning of a lesson to create interest, but tell members that you do not want them to answer the question at this point. At various points throughout the lesson you might refer to the question. Then, as a part of applying the Bible to life, you can ask them to share their answers at the conclusion of the lesson. I have included some other examples at the end of this chapter.

What Kind of Questions Should You Ask?

Questions, like people, come in all shapes and sizes. Some questions are simple. Some are quite complex. Some can be answered in a single word. ("Do you want more ice cream?") Others can take volumes. ("What stages of development has ice cream passed through to get to where it is today?") Some can be phrased so they cannot be answered. ("Can God make more ice cream than He can eat?") Some can be phrased so that, no matter how you answer, you say something you do not want to admit. ("Have you stopped eating too much ice cream?")

In constructing questions, teachers need to be careful to ask the right questions in the right way. Questions should accomplish the following objectives:

- They should help class members understand the lesson.
- They should further the teaching goal or aim.
- They should help class members discover truth for themselves.

- They should be simple without any hidden agenda.
- They should be answerable within the time limit of the class.
- They should add variety to the lesson.

Questions can be asked at several levels. You can ask a simple recall question. (What is the name of Jesus' brother who led the church at Jerusalem?) You can ask a question that calls for a certain degree of understanding. (What was the relationship between Jesus and His brother James?) You can ask questions that make the person analyze certain events or ideas. (Why was it necessary to have Jesus born in one way and James born in another?) You can ask questions that require answers that show the class members have taken the teaching into their lives and accepted (or rejected) it. (What significance does the virgin birth have for your life?)

Each of these questions has its place in helping members to discover truth for themselves. However, questions that make people analyze and evaluate ideas will do much more toward helping people discover truth. However, not all questions can fit into this category.

With a little thought, even questions that call for simple recall can contribute to discovering truth. Just don't ask the obvious. ("Who created the world?") Use questions where the answer is not so obvious. ("Why do you think God created the world?")

How Should You Use Questions?

You can ask questions in almost as many different ways as there are flavors of ice cream. The best word of advice is not to use the same method all the time. Never let your class members become so familiar with your method that they can predict when you will use a particular method. As far as I'm concerned, turkey curry is the most delicious meal I have ever eaten. However, even I would not want turkey curry all the time. Nor do your class members want you to use the same methods or pattern of teaching all the time. Vary the way you ask questions.

Let me suggest several ways you can vary your use of questions. As a general guideline, reverse the way you normally ask questions. This provides just a little twist that can create interest without requiring a lot of work on your part.

Answers and Questions

One way of doing this is to use "Answers and Questions." Print the answers and questions on different color strips of paper. Number the answers, but not the questions. Distribute the questions to one group and the answers to another group. Then let the person with the first answer read the answer and see if the person who has the corresponding question can match it. This activity seems to work better if you do not have more than five or six questions.

Of course, you can also use the more traditional method of giving out questions and answers. However, try answers and questions to create a little more interest.

Scripture Reference: Acts 2:1-47

ANSWERS

1. day of Pentecost
2. sound like a strong wind and tongues like fire
3. disciples spoke in languages of the people
4. a miracle of hearing and speaking
5. Peter

QUESTIONS

What Jewish festival was being celebrated in Acts 2?

What two physical phenomena accompanied the experience at Pentecost?

What was the immediate result of the experience at Pentecost?

What kind of miracle could we say this experience was?

Which disciple explained this miracle to the crowd?

Reverse

Another variation of "Answers and Questions" is what Mic Morrow calls *Reverse*. On a chalkboard or large sheet of paper write answers for which the class will make up questions based on the biblical text. Write the answers one at a time and let the class make up a question that would go with the answer. In the following examples, possible questions are given in parentheses.

Scripture Reference: Genesis 35:1-7,10-13

1. Beth-el (Where did God tell Jacob to go?)
2. An altar (What was Jacob to build at Bethel?)
3. "Put away," "be clean," and "change" (What were three things Jacob told his household to do?)
4. "Who answered me . . . and was with me." (What did Jacob say about God?)
5. Hid them (What did Jacob do with the idols and earrings?)
6. Terror of God (Why did the surrounding cities not pursue Jacob?)
7. Elbethel (What did Jacob call the place where he built an altar?)
8. Israel (What was Jacob's new name?)
9. "I am God Almighty." (How did God identify Himself?)
10. A command and three promises (What was "Be fruitful and multiply," "a nation and a company of nations shall be of thee," "kings shall come out of thy loins," "the land . . . to thee I will give it"?)[2]

Twenty Questions

Play "Twenty Questions." Go through the material you are studying and make up twenty questions. After you have created interest in the lesson, use these twenty questions as a way of guiding Bible study. You may ask these yourself or distribute them to members and let them read the questions and answer them. A third option would be to put them on an overhead cel or large sheet of paper. Use a combination of questions that call for factual information, personal opinion, and life-centered responses. As often as possible, try to draw the information from the biblical text so members can find the answers in their Bibles. If you are using a quarterly or other study book, you can draw information from it, too. That way members would have to search their Bible and quarterly for the answers.

Scripture Reference: John 19:17-37

1. What type of cross did Jesus bear? (19:17)
2. What was the name of the place where Jesus was crucified? (19:17)
3. Why was the place where Jesus was crucified called what it was? (19:17)
4. How many men were crucified that day with Jesus and who might they have been? (19:18)
5. What title did Pilate write and place above Jesus? (19:19)
6. Why was the title written in so many different languages? (19:20)
7. What was the objection of the Jewish leaders to the title placed above Jesus' cross? (19:21)
8. Why do you think Pilate refused to change the title? (19:22)
9. How many soldiers helped crucify Jesus? (19:23)
10. What was unique about Jesus' outer garment? (19:23)
11. How many women stood by Jesus' cross? (19:25)
12. To whom did Jesus commend His mother? (19:26-27)
13. What was the significance of providing this care for His mother? (19:26-27)
14. What two words or expressions from the cross did John record? (19:28,30)
15. Why did the Jewish leaders not want Jesus' body left on the cross after sundown? (19:31)

16. Why did breaking the legs of the victims on the cross hasten their deaths? (19:32-33)
17. Why did the soldiers not break Jesus' legs? (19:33)
18. What Old Testament Scriptures were fulfilled in the actions of the soldiers? (19:36-37)
19. How does Jesus' death on the cross provide atonement?
20. What is the significance of Jesus' death on the cross for you?

Tape questions on the backs of chairs, place them in sealed envelopes, or let members draw them out of a hat or a pile of questions on the table. Sometimes you may even want to let the group trade questions with each other before they answer them or share the questions with others (like you do with gag gifts at a party). Just be careful not to let any kind of trade take more time than it is worth. Remember that your purpose is to get members to discover the truths of the Bible. Finding a creative way to present your questions is only the vehicle you want to use to transport your cargo. Don't let the means become more important than the end you are trying to accomplish.

If you feel daring, let class members make up the questions and ask you! Ask each person to write out one question that deals with the lesson you have been studying. The question can be about the Bible background or the application. Let them give the questions to a member of the class, and let that member ask you the questions. If you answer all the questions, the class has to take you to get ice cream after church!

You can also use biblical skits for asking questions. Consider the following skit based on one of the postresurrection experiences of Jesus.

Lovest Thou Me More Than These?

Scripture reference: John 21:15-18

Voices: 3
Time: 2:15
Narrator: So when they had dined, Jesus saith to Simon
    Peter,
Jesus: Simon, son of Jonah, lovest thou me more than
    these?
Peter: Yea, Lord; thou knowest that I love thee.
Jesus: Feed my lambs.
Narrator: He saith to him again the second time,
Jesus: Simon, son of Jonah, lovest thou me?
Narrator: He saith unto him,
Peter: Yea, Lord; thou knowest that I love thee.
Narrator: He saith unto him,
Jesus: Feed my sheep.
Narrator: He saith unto him the third time,
Jesus: Simon, son of Jonah, lovest thou me?
Narrator: Peter was grieved because he said unto him the
    third time, Lovest thou me? And he said unto him,
Peter: Lord, thou knowest all things; thou knowest that I
    love thee.
Narrator: Jesus saith unto him,
Jesus: Feed my sheep.
Narrator: And He said again,
Jesus: Jim, son of Ed, lovest thou Me more than these?
Jim: But, Lord, what do You mean by love? And what do
    You mean by these things? I could give many an-
    swers to that question. I would like to respond, but
    Your question is just too vague. Could You be more
    specific?
Jesus: Jim, son of Ed, lovest thou Me more than these?
Jim: Well, Lord, haven't You given us all these things.
    Your Word itself says that God looked around at all
    that He had made and said that it was good. Why
    should it be wrong then to collect those good things?
    I am just admiring those things which God has made.
    What's wrong with that?

Jesus: Jim, son of Ed, lovest thou Me more than these?

Jim: But . . . but . . . . no, Lord . . . I cannot honestly say that I love You more than all these other things. But I can say I *want* to love You more than all these other things. That much I can claim. Will You help me?

Here is another variation you can use. Go through the Scripture passage you are studying and make up fifteen to twenty questions. Divide the questions into two or more groups. Try to be sure the questions in each group are of equal difficulty. Write each question on a small card (a three-by-five-inch card works well). Write the answer on the back of the card. Tape each group of cards to a strip of paper that is about four inches wide and three feet long. Use double-sided tape or make loops out of masking tape to affix the cards to the paper. Mount these strips on the wall of your classroom.

Divide the class into as many groups as you have strips of questions. Let each group choose a question to answer. If the group cannot answer it, the other group gets the opportunity.

A variation of this would be to let each group make up questions to ask the other groups. Having to make up the questions would force them into even more discovery learning.

Biblical Questions

Scripture: Genesis 6:9—8:14

GROUP 1

1. Name the three characteristics Noah had that made him attractive to God? (just or righteous, perfect or blameless in his day, walked with God)
2. Why did God say He was going to destroy the earth? (corrupt and filled with violence)
3. What was the inside of the ark covered with? (pitch or tar)

4. How wide was the window around the top of the ark? (18 inches)
5. How long did it rain? (forty days and nights)
6. Who where the people on board the ark? (Noah, his three sons, and each of their wives; eight in all)
7. How long did the water cover the earth? (150 days)
8. What was the first bird Noah sent out? (raven)
9. What was the first thing Noah did after he got off the ark? (built an altar)
10. What did Noah offer on the altar? (one of each of the clean animals and birds)

GROUP 2
1. What were the names of Noah's three sons? (Ham, Shem, Japheth)
2. Of what kind of wood was the ark made? (gopher wood)
3. What was the size of the ark (450 feet long, 75 feet wide, 45 feet high)
4. Why did God not destroy Noah? (because of the covenant)
5. How many of each animal did God instruct Noah to take into the ark? (seven pairs of the clean animals, two pairs of everything else)
6. How long was Noah in the ark before it started raining? (seven days)
7. What were the two sources of water for the flood? (fountains of the deep and floodgates of the sky)
8. How deep was the water on the earth? (25 feet above the mountains)
9. What did the dove bring back to Noah? (olive branch)
10. What was God's reaction to Noah's sacrifice? (promised never to curse the ground or destroy every living creature)

Some General Guidelines for Using Questions

In conclusion, let me share some general guidelines for using questions. When you ask questions, don't answer them yourself. Give the members time to answer the questions. If you have not asked a lot of questions previously, it may take a while for the class to respond to your questions. They may not be quite sure you intend for them to participate, so they may just sit for a while. However, you can convince them that you are serious by waiting for their response.

In phrasing your questions, be sure they cannot be answered with a one-word response. You have not accomplished much if you get a member to answer yes or no. You have not led that member to discover much if only a one-word response is all he or she has to give.

What do you do if a member gives a wrong answer to a question? First, determine if the question could have more than one answer. Of course, if someone responds to the question "What must one do to be born again?" by saying one must join a church and do a lot of good deeds, you would want to correct that statement lest the person and the rest of the class get the wrong answer.

When you encounter an obviously wrong answer that needs correcting, be diplomatic. You might respond something like this: "Thanks for your response, but I'm not sure I agree with you. Let me tell you why." Then you can proceed to give the correct answer.

Members also need to know that they can ask you questions as you teach without fear of being put down or interrupting the class. My attitude has always been that I would rather answer a question a class member has rather than talk for one minute about something no one may be interested in. Just one word of caution: be sure you do not let the group distract you from your primary purpose. If you have a teaching goal or aim, you can determine if the question fits into that framework. If the question doesn't fit, then suggest that you would like to answer it at a later time. Then, keep your promise and come back to it as soon as you can.

Plan the questions that you will use in your lesson just like you plan for the other teaching procedures. Of course, you will think of questions to ask during the lesson, but do give some thought in your preparation to the questions. That way you will be able to use the questions to the best advantage in helping your class members discover God's truth.

How Do Questions Help in Discovery Learning?

How do questions rate in discovery learning? High! Questions are an excellent way to help people discover truth for themselves. When teachers ask questions, they are not telling those in their classes something. Instead, they are getting people to discover something for themselves. Discovering is much more memorable and interesting.

You can use questions in the various forms mentioned. How you use the questions doesn't make as much difference as that you use them. The questions need to be thought out and offered in a variety of ways. They also need to deal with as many of the different levels of learning as possible. Some of the questions of necessity need to deal with recalling basic facts. Others should deal with comprehension and application. However, to make the most out of using questions, you should phrase your questions so they make members analyze, synthesize, and evaluate. When you force members to do this, you are making them look at the Scriptures in light of their life and their conduct. You cannot force people to change their lives. However, you can place them in such a position that they must either examine their lives and their conduct, or they must consciously refuse to do so.

When you use questions that deal with analyzing, synthesizing, and evaluating, you keep people from just memorizing the Bible's facts without considering what those facts mean. Questions that make members examine their lives will help bring about the change in their lives that the Lord would like to see.

I went to a jail service one Sunday afternoon. Much to my surprise, inside the cell was a large sheet of paper on which a prisoner had scrawled the words: "Study to shew thyself approved unto God, a workman that needeth not to be ashamed. 2 Tim. 2:15." I never learned why the man who had written these words was in jail, but I have often thought that here was a man who knew the Bible enough to quote it but did not know enough of it to keep himself out of jail!

God intends for us to do more than just quote the Bible. He wants us to make the Bible a part of our lives, so it influences every aspect of our behavior. Good, well-phrased questions that lead members to examine their lives considering the Bible's great truths can go a long way toward helping people live their lives in the world. It might even keep a few of them out of jail!

4
Let's Talk About This

I visited a Sunday School class taught by a husband and wife team. Each sat behind a desk in front of the class. Easter was just two weeks away, and the lesson was on the cross. The husband began first and spoke for three or four minutes. Then the wife did the same. The husband made additional remarks. Then his wife added a few more comments. Then the husband said, "Now, what does the cross mean to you?" I glanced at my watch. We still had thirty minutes to go! So for thirty minutes we had a group discussion about the cross? No, for thirty minutes we pooled our ignorance. We had a glorified bull session. This was one of the poorest Sunday School classes I have visited.

About this same time I visited another Sunday School class. There were about ten men present. The teacher introduced the lesson, and then for forty-five minutes he "directed traffic." There was never any question about who was in charge. He asked questions. He made statements. He offered clarification when it was necessary. When we needed to move on, he would introduce another part of the lesson. The teacher was "directing" the discussion. The class was one of the most stimulating Sunday School classes I have been in.

What made the difference? Both classes involved the teacher(s) making a presentation at the beginning of the class to set the stage. Both classes involved about thirty minutes of discussion.

What made the difference between the two classes? In the second example, the teacher *guided* a group discussion. He remained in control. He was still at the helm. He knew where he wanted us to come out. The discussion was not aimless. When we finished, he knew whether we had accomplished the aim he had in mind for us at the beginning. The teacher used group discussion as a teaching method to accomplish his teaching aim or goal.

In the first example, the teachers did not have any particular goal in mind. They did not guide the discussion. It was haphazard. The teachers did not have an aim. They did not know where they wanted to lead the class. They used group discussion as a way to fill up a block of time.

Let's see if we can discover some guidelines that will help us use group discussion to the best of our abilities. Group discussion is another of the basic teaching methods. Most teachers make some use of it at some point. It may be done poorly, or it may be done in an exciting manner. It is a great method to help class members discover God's truth for themselves. However, it can also be a cop-out for lack of preparation and poor planning. It can make a boring class, or it can lead members to new depths of insight.

Haven't We Discussed This Before?

Have you ever been in a Sunday School class and suddenly felt like you had heard the discussion before? Bill Schwartzenberger is sounding off again on his favorite topic. Bonnie Butterfield is waiting to get her word in edgewise or any other way she can—except it's the same word(s) she spoke last week, and the week before that.

Is this group discussion? No. Dealing with a subject is

always easier if we know what the subject is. Group discussion is not just letting class members talk about whatever they want to talk about.

Often teachers of youth let the members manipulate them into talking about Friday night's football game, the party the night before, or some other topic. The teachers give in on the assumption that the youth will like them better if they will let them talk about something they want.

My contention is that the Bible speaks to the lives of youth (and everybody else!), and they need to study it. Bible study does not have to be dull. It can be interesting —even for youth! Youth can find other people to talk to about football and dating, but few will talk to them about God's Word. By this I do not mean that we should not relate the Bible to their lives. That is an absolute necessity. However, we do not have to let them manipulate us. That is exactly what they do not need.

Group discussion is not even letting members talk about the lesson and share their views about it. If it were a secular topic we would call that a bull session.

Group discussion is a teaching method by which the teacher *leads* the class toward a particular aim or goal. The teacher guides the discussion; it is not just an opportunity for class members to say anything they wish. The teacher plans what takes place; the discussion does not just happen. It has a purpose; it is not just getting members to wake up and talk.

When Should You Use Group Discussion?

As with any teaching method, group discussion works better in some situations than in others.

Use group discussion when the group has the background to handle the topic they are discussing. It would be rather useless to discuss the influence of Aramaic on the Greek Gospels with a group that has not yet learned how to read the Gospels in English. However, that group might have the capabilities to discuss how the Gospels apply to their lives. A good discussion must be built on the basic assumption that the group members doing the discussing have a certain level of knowledge, so they can participate. Generally speaking, topics that involve feelings and attitudes can be used with most groups. Topics that require a certain level of knowledge must be chosen more carefully.

Use group discussion when you want to involve the whole group. Discussion by its very nature is a way to get people involved. This means that the group has to be a certain size. Group discussion is difficult with more than twelve to fifteen members. However, even in larger groups, you can ask members to turn to a person or persons next to them and discuss a topic for a few minutes and then report back to the group. If the group is small enough, you can involve all the members in a guided discussion.

Use group discussion when you feel secure in your teaching role. Teachers expose themselves to a certain amount of risk when they open the class to group discussion. Teachers who are not sure of their role do not use group discussion. It is much safer and more comfortable to be in charge. When a teacher is giving a straight lecture, members have little time to question statements or raise issues. Only those teachers who feel assured of themselves will use group discussion.

Use group discussion with other teaching methods. Seldom will a teacher use only group discussion for a whole lesson. Group discussion works best with other methods. More on this later.

How Should You Prepare for Group Discussion?

As already suggested, group discussion must be planned to be effective. What steps can teachers take?

Know Where You Are Going

When you teach a Bible study or Sunday School lesson, you must know where you are going. I heard of a old man from the mountains who was known far and wide for his expert marksmanship. All over his farm the man had bull's eyes with a rifle shot right in the center. Someone asked him how he was always able to hit the bull's eye right in the center. "It's very simple," he said. "I just shoot and then draw a circle around it."

Many Sunday School teachers teach the way this fellow shot. They don't know where they're going, but when they get there, they just draw a circle around it and say they accomplished their aim. The only person they are fooling is themselves.

The bull's eye comes first. Set a goal or an aim, so you will know whether you have hit anything. What do you want to hit? What do you want to accomplish? Unless you know before you start, you will never know if you accomplished your purpose.

When you get ready to plan a group discussion, you must know where you are going. If not, when you finish, you may have talked for thirty minutes about the cross and never had a group discussion. You will only have let the members talk. That is not teaching.

Know What Road You Will Take to Get There

You must also know what road you will take to get there. It is possible to go from Nashville to Louisville by way of Birmingham, but it sure is a long way out of the way. If my goal is to drive directly to Louisville, I would never plan to go through Birmingham. If my purpose is just to drive, I might choose to go through Birmingham. It all depends on what my purpose is.

If my goal is to discover how the resurrection can make my life more significant, then I know when someone starts talking about Jesus turning water into wine that I as the discussion leader must cut it off and get the discussion back on track.

Stay on the Right Road

Be sure you keep the group on track. Don't let the group be like a ride on a roller coaster. The ride may be exciting (I don't think so; I even get woozy watching a film made from a roller coaster), but you get off the same place you got on. You have not made any progress.

Use some kind of outline to keep the group headed in the right direction. Don't let the discussion double back on itself, so you find yourself going over the same territory you have previously covered. Place an outline on a large sheet of paper or on the chalkboard or overhead cel. As you cover one point, move on to the next. This way you are heading someplace.

Watch Out for the Potholes

The road on which a group discussion travels is full of potholes. If you are aware of them, you can avoid them. One pothole you should watch out for is to keep one person from dominating the discussion. Some people like to try to impress others with their great knowledge, so they talk. Others get started and don't know how to stop, so they talk. Others talk for different reasons. Whatever the reason, you must not allow one person to dominate the discussion. You can do this sometimes by breaking into the monologue and thanking the person. Then ask someone else a question or change the topic or procedure.

If that doesn't work, you may need to approach the person privately. Explain that you appreciate the contributions (if you do) that the person has made, but you would like to try to get some of the other members in the class to participate. Then ask the person to do a sociogram for you. A sociogram is a diagram of the room with a circle drawn where each person is sitting. Each time a person talks, a line is drawn from the person who talks to the person to whom he is talking. That will help keep the overactive talker quiet and will also let him see how many times he himself enters into the discussion.

Another pothole to avoid is letting the group get sidetracked. The story is told at The Southern Baptist Theological Seminary in Louisville, Kentucky, that a student appeared in class one day with a shotgun. When the professor strayed from his lecture, the student rose and brandished the gun. "What are you doing?" cried the professor. "I am trying to shoot that rabbit you have been chasing."[1] Sunday School teachers must be careful not to let the class get sidetracked. You may need to shoot some of the rabbits members will attempt to chase.

Don't let the quiet member get lost. Some members will sit and never say a word in a group discussion. You can involve them by asking questions they can answer. Your goal should be to get all the members to participate, not just to occupy the time by having members talk.

Be Sure You Have Enough Fuel to Get There

Some topics work great for a group discussion. Others do not have enough substance in them. When you choose a topic for a group discussion, be sure you have enough fuel to get you to where you want to go. If you plan an hour's group discussion on why Jesus asked Peter three times if he loved Him (John 21:15-17), you might have some problems. However, if you plan a group discussion on what things we love more than we love Jesus and how we can love Jesus more than everything else, you should be able to build a good lesson. Whatever topic you choose, just be sure it has enough content to carry the dis cussion so you won't run out of gas before you finish your journey.

Whatever the topic is, you must be prepared. Group discussion is not an excuse to keep from studying. You must know whether the comments your members make are accurate. If not, the class members may leave with misinformation. You must know all you can about a given passage of Scripture. You must have a certain amount of knowledge to phrase the questions that the class will use in the discussion. You must know what the Scripture says so you will know what to aim for.

Be Sure That Where You're Going Is Worth Going To

If you're planning a group discussion, be sure that the topic you choose is worth discussing. You might be able to get a discussion going on the theological implications of the good Samaritan's use of a donkey or where Cain got his wife, but so what? Who cares? What difference would it make if you knew? Many topics discussed in Sunday School classes and Bible study groups just do not make any difference. I saw a Joe Mckeever cartoon recently that showed the preacher saying: "The first word in this verse is 'the.' Let us look more closely at the use of this word . . ." A person in the audience is saying, "I love in-depth Bible studies."

You could discuss some topics for several hours and not contribute to the spiritual lives of your class members or to their understanding of God's Word. Any time you plan a group discussion, be sure the topic you choose will add and value to the lives of your class members.

Be Sure It's the Best Way to Get There

I can go from my house to church in over a dozen different ways. Depending on traffic conditions, time of day, how much time I have, what mood I'm in, whether certain houses have flowers in bloom, I choose a different way. All the ways are about the same distance, but some take less time if the traffic is heavy.

You can teach a Bible lesson using many different teaching methods. When you use group discussion, be sure that it is the best way to get to where you want to go. Be certain that you cannot present the material better using a lecture, case studies, or some other method. Let the subject dictate what method you use.

Some General Guidelines for Group Discussion

In some respects, group discussion is like all other teaching methods. However, it has some special considerations.

How Long Should the Discussion Last?

To ask how long a group discussion should last fits in the same category as asking how long a piece of string should be. It all depends. A piece of string to tie around your finger doesn't have to be nearly as long as a piece of string to tie around a big box.

Some group discussions need not be more than five or six minutes in length. Other group discussions can be an hour long. The length should be governed by several aspects: (1) What do you want to accomplish? (2) What knowledge do your members have of the subject? (3) How important is the subject to the lives of your members? (4) How much time do you have available? All these aspects would influence how long a discussion should be.

Where Should Discussion Come in the Lesson?

Group discussion can come at just about any point in

the lesson. You can use a discussion to introduce a topic and create interest. To introduce a lesson on Luke 20:19-26, write the following on the chalkboard: churches should pay taxes. As members enter, ask them to form groups of three and discuss this among themselves and be prepared to share a report with the rest of the group.

If you want to use group discussion to study the Bible passage, you could do that, too. You could approach it in at least two different ways. First, you could discuss the following questions as a group: (1) What Jewish groups sought to trick Jesus and why? (2) Why was the taxation issue such an inflammable topic in Jesus' day? (3) What was Jesus' answer, and how did the Jewish leaders respond? A second approach would be to divide the class into three groups, let them work individually on these questions, and then report to the whole group.

You can also use discussion to help the members of your group apply the Scripture to their lives. Group discussion works well to help members pull together the biblical material and see how it applies to their lives. To help members do that with this passage of Scripture, ask: What principles did Jesus lay down in His answer? How do those principles apply to Christians today?

Group discussion works particularly well in applying the Bible to our lives. Discussion can help members identify their attitudes about particular topics and identify ways they can change those attitudes.

Group discussion can be used at any point in a lesson or Bible study. It just needs to be tailored to the particular area that you are trying to develop.

How Large Should Discussion Groups Be?

Group discussion can take place with any group that has more than one person in it. Naturally, a group of two or a group of fifty would require a little different approach.

If you have a small group of four to six, you probably would want to include the whole group in any discussion. However, even that small number can be divided into two groups to discuss different topics and then share a report with the group.

If you have a large group of more than twelve to fifteen, it becomes difficult to have a group discussion in which all the group participates. In large groups, you may want to ask them to turn to the person next to them and discuss the assigned topic and then share their decisions with the whole group.

Group discussion can be used with any size group; you just need to compensate for groups that are small or large.

How Do You Get a Discussion Started?

Teachers often complain that they cannot get a discussion started. What can you do to get people to participate in a discussion?

The most important point is to be sure that the topic you want to discuss relates to their lives. The topic "Churches should pay taxes" would get their attention and relate to their lives. If a topic relates to their daily lives, group members will be much more likely to share some kind of response. You can also ask for specific answers. If your group has not been accustomed to group discussion, begin by asking for personal feelings about a specific topic. General questions that relate to how the Scriptures apply to life probably work best in this case. Such questions as the following should give you an idea: What is the most difficult aspect about living the Christian life? What makes living the Christian life worthwhile? How has the Bible helped you to get through a difficult time in your life? Have you ever had a prayer answered? What can you do to avoid being tempted?

What one practice have you found that improved your prayer life? When discussion questions relate to their lives, members will be much more likely to respond.

Be careful that you do not put anyone down who shares an answer. Jim Wilcoxon was teaching his men's Sunday School class. He had just attended a conference on how to improve his teaching, so he thought he would try to have some group discussion. He asked what Jesus meant when He said that we were the salt of the earth (Matt. 5:13). Bill Blevins spoke up and said he thought it meant that we should add flavor and meaning to life. Jim responded by saying, "No, Bill, you're wrong. What Jesus had in mind was the ability of Christians to preserve society as salt preserves meat."

Do you think Bill shared much more in the group discussion? Not unless he was a very strong person! Be careful about squelching members by the way you respond to their answers. Here, there could have been more than one answer. Both Bill and Bob were right. In other cases, the person may not be right. However, unless it involves a serious doctrinal error, avoid telling people they are wrong. Always try to thank the person for the answer, even though it may not be what you had in mind. Your acceptance of that person's response may be more important than the answer to the question.

An important element in encouraging discussion is the way the people sit in the classroom. If the chairs are in a circle or around a table so all the group can see each other's face, then you are much more likely to get them to discuss. It is hard to comment on what people have to say if you are looking at the back of their heads.

The Relationship to Other Teaching Methods

Group discussion fits in well with other teaching methods. It adds variety and increases the interest level over using a single method.

Lecture

A brief lecture can be followed by a group discussion to be certain that you have covered all the points you had intended and to be certain that the group heard what you thought you said. Before the lecture you can divide the group into smaller groups and make some listening assignments. Then after you have presented the lecture, let the groups discuss their assignments and then share a summary of their discussion. If your class is not large, you can do this as a single group.

Questions

Group discussion also works well with questions. You can build your teaching plan on several questions and then use these as the basis of a discussion. In a lesson on Job 38:1—42:17 about God's appearing to Job in the whirlwind, the following points of discussion could be raised: (1) Discuss what God's appearance to Job says about God's involvement in human suffering. (2) Discuss what changes occur in a person's life when that person encounters God. (3) Discuss how friends can support someone in the midst of sorrow and conflict.

These questions could be printed on a large sheet of paper or a chalkboard and used as a basis for a class discussion, or they could be printed on smaller pieces of paper and given to members or groups.

Case Studies

Case studies especially work well with group discussion. You can read a case study and then ask the group what the person did right or wrong, or what the person should have done that was not done. Just be sure you have enough information in your case study to give members all the facts they will need to make a decision. You could use the following case study to introduce a lesson on Job: "John's business had failed, and he had lost most of his money. Shortly after this, his only son was killed in a car accident. The day following the funeral, John had a heart attack. You have gone to the hospital to visit John. As you talk, he says, 'Why did God allow this to happen to me?' You say . . ."[2]

You can use other types of case studies that give a whole situation. Mary Beth was only thirty-two when she died from a rare form of cancer. She had not been ill long, but she still had run up a lot of medical bills. Her husband, Brian, and their two children, ages nine and five, had moved to the city only a short time before from a different part of the country. They had no family in the area, and both Brian's and Mary Beth's parents lived several hundred miles away. They had joined First Suburban Church but had not been too active because of Mary Beth's illness. After the funeral, someone in the Sunday School requested prayer for Brian and the children. Someone else spoke up and said, "Can't we do more than pray for them? I think we need to do that, but I think Brian and the children need more than that right now?"

This kind of case study can be followed by a group discussion on such points as: (1) What can a Sunday School class do to help Brian? (2) What can a Sunday School class do to help the children? (3) What can be done immediately? (4) What can be done long term? (5) What resources would be available to the Sunday School class to use to help the family?

This kind of discussion lifts the conversation from the theoretical to the practical. It keeps the discussion from being aimless.

Other Methods

Other methods relate well to group discussion. You can use role play in much the same way as you would case studies. A role play is a portrayal of a modern event acted out by class members. After the role play, present certain questions to the group to serve as a guide for discussion. As an example, the above case study about Brian and Mary Beth could be made into a role play. The same questions could be used to guide the group discussion.

Biblical skits, biblical simulations, monologues, and drama all can be followed by group discussion. Just be sure you have certain questions planned to guide the discussion. You as the teacher are the catalyst. You must guide the discussion, or it becomes meaningless.

How Does Group Discussion Help in Discovery Learning?

By now you have probably guessed that group discussion is a great way to help members of your group discover biblical truths for themselves. Group discussion works well because members talk about what they feel and are learning. The method also enables teachers to check up to see what their members are hearing and thinking.

Group discussion gives you an opportunity to guide what members examine. By determining in advance certain topics you want them to consider, you are able to expose your class members to certain thoughts, ideas, and Scriptures.

Group discussion and discovery learning go hand in glove. By using group discussion you can lead your class to discover biblical truths for themselves.

5
Did You Ever Ride the Bull?

Several years ago it was popular to ride a mechanical bull that jumped, turned, and twisted. It was possible to set the jumping, turning, and twisting at the speed the rider felt comfortable in handling—from slow to suicide. You really did not ride a bull (you didn't have to feed him or take care of him!), but it was the next thing to it. Case studies are like that. They take people out of the stands, put them on the bull, and give them a similar experience without all the involvement. (No, I never rode the bull! I only read about it: sort of like a case study of a case study where you can sample the sample. As far as I'm concerned that's close enough to that experience for me.)

"A certain man went down from Jerusalem to Jericho" (Luke 10:30). Does this story sound familiar? I hope so! It is the beginning of Jesus' parable of the good Samaritan. It is also an excellent example of Jesus' use of a case study. Jesus painted a verbal picture of an event and plunged His listeners directly into the midst of having to make decisions. Jesus was a master in using case studies. The Gospels are full of examples.

Who Wants to Study Cases?

Why should anyone want to study a case? What kind of case will we study? A piano case? A criminal case? A glasses case? What can studying cases do to make Bible study more interesting? It all depends on what kind of cases you study!

The kind of cases I have in mind are brief histories or stories about people and the problems they encounter. They can be quite brief—as is the parable of the good Samaritan—or they can be more complete. A case study must have enough details about a particular event that the class can understand the event and make some kind of decision about it.

Leroy Ford, in his book on case studies,[1] lists twelve different types or varieties of case studies. Although the varieties are different, they all have similar characteristics. The case study presents a problem for the group to deal with, and then the group arrives at a solution.

Examples of Case Studies

Let me share with you some basic types of case studies that you can use to help class members discover how the Bible applies to life.

The most basic form is the *complete* case study. This can be a short story or paragraph that gives enough information for the group to make a decision. The following is a paragraph out of an article in the newspaper. Although it is just part of the whole article, it offers enough of a problem for members to debate a significant moral issue.

"Phone companies face a difficult decision when it comes to the issue of dial-a-porn. Pretend you're the company president. Which option would you choose? Allow sex-talk into the system and reap what could be millions of dollars in profits—or rebates for customers. Turn down the phone-sex purveyors and risk being taken to court where a protracted legal battle can cost thousands of dollars, a cost shared by the common consumer."[2]

Another kind of case study that you can use is what I like to call a *life situation.* This variety presents a dilemma and breaks into the event before the answer is given and asks the group to supply the answer. Usually, the situation can have many possible answers. I like to tie life situations in with certain Scriptures. See if you can determine the Scripture behind this one.

"Joe met Pam when he first started working at her father's store. They had talked some at the store when Pam called Joe and invited him to a party at her house. When he knocked, Pam met him at the door and ushered him into the den. She looked beautiful. It took Joe a minute to realize that no one else was around. He was rather confused, but he enjoyed being alone with her. After talking for a while, Pam came over and sat down in his lap. 'My parents are gone for the weekend,' she said. 'We have the whole house to ourselves. Come on upstairs to the bedroom.'

"Joe was shaken. He tried to explain to Pam that he liked her a lot, but he could not have sex with her. When he continued to refuse, Pam said, 'If you don't, I'll tell the police that you tried to rape me.'

"Joe said . . ."[3]

A third variety is the *picture* case study. Instead of reading a story, show a picture and ask members what is going on in the picture. Ask them how they would respond if they were a certain person in the picture.

A picture in a magazine shows a small boy holding a baseball bat standing in front of a broken window. Towering over him is a middle-aged man holding a baseball. If you teach children, you can ask them what they would do or say in this situation. If you teach adults, you can ask them how they would respond. Ask how they would want the adult to respond if they were the boy. Then ask if there is any difference in their response. If so, why?

Often *comic strips* or *cartoons* can be used to introduce a serious topic. As you read and discover items that can be related to the Scripture, clip these and file them for future use.

Television programs can also serve as a basis for case studies. The following is based loosely on the television movie: *Celebration Family*. Ross and Martha had adopted twelve children who were handicapped either emotionally or physically. Some of the neighbors began to complain about having the children in the community. A neighbor comes to your door circulating a petition saying that the children are not getting the care they should be getting. You know of some incidents in which the children have had some problems, but you also know that Ross and Martha are good parents and love their children. When the neighbor asks you to sign the petition to get the children taken away, you say . . .

Why Use Case Studies?

Using case studies sounds like a lot of trouble. Why even bother with using them? What advantage are they? What good do they do?

Case studies paint pictures for people. They get people involved. They make people place themselves in situations where they have to make decisions. That's why Jesus' parables are so attractive and interesting. They reach out and grab people and pull them into the story. Jesus' parables are all so believable. Even though the cultural atmosphere has changed greatly, most of Jesus' parables are still as significant to us as they were to the people of the first century. Which of us has not "passed by on the other side" (Luke 10:31) when we were too busy, afraid, or just indifferent?

We cannot participate in every kind of experience, but we can get a little taste of how we would act by reading and responding to a case study. Case studies make us think; they get us involved. Even though they are not real to us (although they may have been real to someone else), they can help us learn how to respond to real situations.

When Do You Use Case Studies?

Case studies are also like ice cream—they are good any-time. Few teaching methods can create interest faster or more thoroughly than a good case study. Let me give you some examples of how you can use case studies.

To Create Interest in Bible Study

Case studies create interest as well as any method. Listen to public speakers. Often preachers will begin their sermons with illustrations that capture your interest. Then they can move on to lay out the Bible's claims.

Case studies do this same thing in the class room. Don't assume that just because people have come to Sunday School that they are interested in studying the Bible. That is not so. You need something to create interest. You can use other teaching methods to grab members' attention, but case studies work exceptionally well. Case studies give you the opportunity to bring up an issue that deals with the lives of class members. When you start with something that is a problem in members' lives, you are much more likely to earn a hearing for the study of the Bible.

Few people are interested in a study of the Bible just for the sake of studying the Bible. Most people want to know how it applies to their lives. A frequent question they ask —and, therefore, so should teachers—is: So what? Who cares just about biblical information? Most people want to know how that information applies to their lives. The Bible was written for that purpose. It shows us how to live in relationship with God and others. As a Bible teacher, you have the opportunity to help members discover the great truths of the Bible and how those truths apply to their lives.

Case studies help you do this because they deal with current issues people face every day. Case studies that deal with the basic issues we face will catch the interest of the group. Family relationships, moral decisions, relationships on the job or in school are examples of issues your class members deal with. The following is an example of a case study to begin a lesson on how to live harmoniously with God and others. The lesson is based on Psalm 133:1-3.

"Two brothers had grown up in a middle-class home with most of the things they wanted that all their friends had. They were close to each other and had a good relationship with their parents. When they entered college, one began to do better in his studies than the other, and the parents showed a slight favoritism for the first time. The relationship worsened to the point that the other brother dropped out of school and went to work in a dead-end job. The one who stayed in school graduated and started a job with good potential for the future. He did well and received promotions. The parents continued to use him as a example to the brother who had not done well. Needless to say, relationships between the brothers and the parents were not too harmonious."[4]

Anyone who has had a brother or sister—or someone else the parents held up as an example—can identify with this example. Regardless of our place in the family, most of us have felt that at some point our parents showed favoritism to the younger or older brother or sister. Whether they did or didn't is immaterial. Our perception influenced the way we felt.

After reading this case study, the teacher can raise several questions. If you teach parents, you could approach the study from the position of what the parents did wrong. What could they have done differently? Why did they do what they did? How could they have accomplished their goal of encouraging the poorer student without creating hostility between the two brothers?

If you teach youth or young adults, you could approach

the study from the position of what the brothers could have done to keep the parents from driving the wedge between them. What could the brothers have said to the parents? What could the brothers have said to each other? What could the brothers do if the parents did not change their approach?

Once you have brought up these questions, you can move to the Bible study itself to find principles in God's Word that speak to these kinds of problems.

To Make Bible Study Purposeful

Case studies can also be used in the midst of the Bible study to give purpose and meaning to it. Think how the following case study can be used to illustrate Matthew 11:28-30. After you have introduced the Scripture and members have read it in their Bibles, read this case study.

Linda was thirty-eight when her husband died. She was left with two boys to raise. She had always been active in church, but in the weeks and months following her husband's death, Linda began to question many things about her faith. Susan, her best friend, asked Linda one day how she was getting along. Linda's anger came tumbling out. She voiced her hostility at God, the church, her friends, and her family. According to Linda, no one cared. Life wasn't fair. God should not have taken her husband and left her with the two boys to raise.

Now, ask the following questions: How can Matthew 11:28-30 provide an answer for Linda? What promises does Jesus make in these verses? How do these verses apply to our daily lives? Can we take Jesus' words literally, or are they symbolic? What other Scripture passages could offer Linda help at this point in her life?

Using case studies to make Bible study more significant will keep members from studying the Bible in a vacuum. Case studies keep members from being detached. Case studies place people in the saddle so they have to struggle with what it is like to ride the wild bull.

To Apply the Bible to Life

Case studies are excellent devices to apply the Bible's message to life.

Jerry had always been a difficult child. His mother had died when he was born, and his father had raised Jerry and his older brother. Jerry never got along with his father or his brother. During his senior year in high school, Jerry joined the army. After having served in the military for four years, Jerry worked at odd jobs all over the country. He said he was "trying to find himself." Jerry got into drugs, and he was arrested for soliciting an undercover police-woman whom he mistook for a prostitute. One day Jerry showed up at the front door of his home. He was penni-less, addicted to drugs, and his health was broken. When Jerry's father and brother answered the door, they said . .

Could you use the above case study to apply a lesson on the prodigal son from Luke 15:11-32? All too easily we accept that the father in Jesus' parable welcomed his son back without any difficulty. However, it is not easy to take back someone in Jerry's shape. That is one point the parable makes. What is so hard for human fathers is the norm for God. God forgives when we cannot.

A case study takes the Scriptures out of the abstract and puts them into a experience that we recognize as a part of our lives today. Case studies enable us to test our belief in the Bible against our behavior.

Are you convinced of the validity and usefulness of case studies? I hope so. They will help you lead your members to discover the truths of God's Word for themselves.

Where Do You Find Case Studies to Use?

You can come up with case studies in several ways. One way is to make them up. The case study about Jerry is made up, yet it really isn't. It is just a retelling of the story Jesus told. I have changed a few minor details, but it is still the same story. In another sense, it is not made up. Jerry's name could have been Bill, Brian, Barbara, or Bonnie. For the experience I have related—with a few variations of details—has been the experience of many parents. So in another sense, it is not made up. It is quite real.

This degree of reality is what makes the story believable. In order for the story to communicate to the class, it must have a ring of authenticity. It must not be so fanciful that it does not sound true.

To test your own ability to construct case studies, turn to Luke 10:30-35. Read through this familiar passage. Then rewrite the scene, setting it in the streets of a large city or along a deserted country road—whichever setting would be most appropriate for your class. Here is my rewrite of the passage. I chose to make it a life situation. "Bob was out visiting for his church on Thursday evening. He had an appointment at 7:30 with a prospective family who had just moved to town. They had attended First Church for the last three Sundays, and Bob was certain they would join in spite of the fact that they had to pass First Suburban Church on the way. He glanced at his watch. He was running late. If he went around by the regular route, he would be late. He could cut through the old part of town and make it. As he drove through the dark streets, he unconsciously locked the doors of the car. As he rounded a curve, his headlights picked up two men bending over a third man who was lying on the sidewalk. When they saw his lights, the two men broke and ran, leaving the third man on the sidewalk. Bob hesitated for a moment, trying to decide what he should do, then he . . ."[5]

If you can learn to construct your own case studies, you will be able to shape them in the exact direction you want to go.

You can also find case studies in newspapers, magazines, and books. Develop the habit of looking for case studies that you can use in your teaching when you read. I took today's paper and looked through it. I found two articles and a comic strip that could be used.

The headline of one article read, "Angry 9-year old girl kills brother, 20." The article went on to tell of a girl who got upset because her older brother reprimanded her and her three brothers for roughhousing. The girl got a knife from the kitchen and stabbed her brother in the chest.[6] This article would make an excellent illustration to begin a lesson on Matthew 5:21-22.

A second article is entitled "Man in White Strikes." A man dressed in a white tuxedo and top hat pulled into the city of Moline, Illinois. The man entered a department store and paid over $400 for merchandise customers were checking out at the cash register. A clerk said customers reacted by asking, "Is he for real?"[7]

This story could be read to create interest in a stewardship lesson. After you have read the case study, ask: If we are faithful in our stewardship, will a man in white come along and pay our bills?

A third article was a comic strip. One man was reading a newspaper article about a TV preacher and remarked that the paper called him a "profit." He turned to a chaplain and asked if that shouldn't be spelled "prophet." The chaplain replied that in the case of that individual they spelled it correctly![8] Surely you can use this in a lesson on Christian life-style, greed, or integrity.

You can also make case studies from your own experience. Earlier, I shared with you when I learned not to throw green apricots at pretty girls in swings after dark. That is an example of a case study drawn from personal experience. Often members will be able to share examples from their experiences as well.

When checking the newspaper or writing your own case studies, don't forget to check the advice columns. Many times letters will appear in them that you can read and ask your class to respond to. You can write a case study in the style of a letter to an advice columnist and let class members respond with their answers.

You can find case studies in the letters to the editor columns—especially in religious papers or magazines. Read the letter and ask the class if they would agree or disagree. You might even let the class compose a response.

Another source of case studies is to have your class write their own. After you have presented the Bible study, divide the class into smaller groups of two or three persons. Ask them how they would apply the Bible to their lives. Let them write a case study that would show how they have understood the lesson. In teaching Luke 15:11-32, divide the class into three groups (a group does not need to have more than one person in it). Ask Group 1 to write a case study from the father's perspective. Ask Group 2 to write a case study from the younger son's perspective. Ask Group 3 to write a case study from the elder brother's perspective. Be sure you have time to let all the groups read their examples.

Case studies are available all around us. Develop an "eye" for them. You will surprise yourself with how many different types you discover.

How to File Case Studies

When you see case studies that can be used, cut them out or make copies of them. Set up a file so you can retrieve them easily. If you have a personal computer, you can set up your file on it. If you do not, you can use regular file folders and 4-by-6-inch cards. Tape each case study to an 8 1/2-by-11-inch sheet of paper so all sheets

will be the same size. At the top of each sheet write (1) the
Scripture references the case study could be used with,
and (2) topics the case study could be used to illustrate.
Assign each item a CSF (Case Study File) number: CSF 1.
On a 4-by-6-inch card write each topic you have written
on a case study you are going to file. Below that heading,
write the number of each item that relates to that topic
and a brief description. The case study about the girl killing her brother could read: CSF 1—Angry girl kills brother. I would file this under the following topics: anger, Ser-
mon on the Mount, murder, and family. The more areas
you file it under, the more likely you are to find it later
and use it.

Besides this topic card, make a separate Scripture reference card for each book of the Bible. On the Matthew
card, write 5:21-22 and write CSF 1 beside it.

Place the article in a file folder numbered CSF 1-25.
When you get twenty-five items in the folder start a new
folder.

When you need a case study on Matthew 5:21-22, you
can pull out the card to see if you have anything on the
subject. Or, if you need a case study on anger, pull out the
topic card labeled **Anger** and then look up all the references you have listed.

This system is quite simple and takes little time to set
up. You can also use it for any other file you want. You
could have a general file (GF), a Sunday School file (SSF),
or any other file you need.

How Do Case Studies Relate to Discovery Learning?

Great! Case studies rank high in helping class members
discover biblical truths for themselves. Few teaching
methods have the latitude of involving members like case
studies. A teacher who uses case studies will involve

members in finding out what the Bible says for themselves. The members will have to think through the Bible's teachings as they deal with the modern situations that the case studies present.

You can involve members by asking someone who does not participate often to read a printed case study to the rest of the class. You can give printed copies to all the members and ask them to answer questions individually. You can let them work in groups, or you can work together as a whole class. However you use the case study, you will be asking members to relate the Bible's message to today. That is the whole purpose of discovery learning. The discovery quotient for case studies is quite high.

How Do Case Studies Relate to Other Methods?

Case studies work well with most other teaching methods. As we have already seen, case studies work well with lecture, group discussion, and questions.

You can ask members to role play case studies instead of reading them. The following case study could be read or role played:

Shortly after John got a divorce, Harold met him on the street. Harold had not seen John since the divorce had been granted. "John, I'm glad to see you. I want you to know that even if you were wrong in getting a divorce, I'll stick by you. I don't care what other people are saying about you, it's not going to affect how I feel about you. Well, I'll see you around. I've got to run. Call me if you need to talk."

After the role play ask what Harold did wrong, what he could have done differently, and how he could have supported John more.

Another way of using case studies is to let different groups make up their own ending to them. The same case study could be modified and made into a life-situation experience:

Shortly after John got a divorce, Harold met him on the street. Harold had not seen John since the divorce had been granted. When he saw him, Harold said . . . Divide the class into several small groups and let them role play their response to the class.

Case studies work well with questions, too. The two methods are hard to separate.

Case studies get high marks in discovery learning. The more you use them, the more your class members will discover biblical truths for themselves. If that is what you want to happen in the lives of your members, you will use case studies.

6
Tell Me What You Think

We have few opportunities to tell someone what we think without being judged, refuted, or poked in the nose! Brainstorming does that—well, sort of. Within the context of the question or problem posed by the leader, brainstorming encourages class members to share ideas without having to be right or have all the answers.

Is Brainstorming Wind Blowing Through an Empty Place?

Some wag has defined a brainstorm as wind blowing through an empty place. Brainstorming can be that if the participants do not follow a few simple guidelines. It can also be an effective way to get people to discover biblical truth for themselves.

Brainstorming is a problem-solving activity that gets people to give rapid-fire responses without stopping to evaluate or comment on the validity of the responses. Then, after all the responses are made, the group evaluates, assigns priorities, or makes some kind of group response to the ideas suggested.

One word of caution. As the teacher, try not to make suggestions during this sharing. If you participate, you defeat the purpose of the activity. You want the group's ideas, not yours. If you have some good ideas, wait until the group has finished. If someone else suggests your idea,

great! If not, you can add one or two ideas to the list when
others have finished.

The Purposes of Brainstorming

Brainstorming has several purposes or functions that
other teaching methods cannot do or cannot do as well.

The primary purpose of brainstorming is to get a lot of
new ideas before the group. Kathy had been trying to get
her Sunday School class members to spend more time in
ministering to members and prospects. In a lesson on
Matthew 25:31-46 she asked, What can we do as a class to
minister to our members and prospects? For the next four
to five minutes the members shared ideas they had that
would help them to meet some of the needs of the people
they knew. Kathy had asked Jackie to write the ideas on a
large sheet of paper, so they could have a list of every suggestion that the group made.

Kathy had thought of several ministries that the class
ought to perform. The members mentioned several excellent ideas that she had not even thought of—some of
which required little time and involvement but would
provide a needed ministry.

Brainstorming worked much better than if Kathy had
prepared a lecture and outlined her ideas. The class had
ideas that Kathy did not have.

Possibly even more important, the class made the suggestions. They would be much more likely to buy into the
ideas when it came time to put the ideas into practice.
This aspect of brainstorming helps the group "own" the
ideas. If you gave them the identical list they suggested,
they would probably not accept the ideas as readily as if
they had thought of them.

Brainstorming also encourages members to participate
in the class. Most people have at least one good idea on
most subjects. However, many people are afraid to share

their ideas. In the climate of brainstorming, they have the freedom to share any idea that relates to the subject.

One of the women in Kathy's class, Gloria, was quiet, but she was quite intelligent and had a lot of good ideas. However, she seldom shared her ideas in group discussion. During the brainstorming session, Gloria suggested that the class send a letter to the parents of each baby born in the local hospital, congratulating them on the birth of their baby, and offering them the spiritual support of the church.

Later, during the evaluation period, the class agreed that this was something they would like to do. Gloria felt affirmed for having made the suggestion. Encouraging participation is a central feature of brainstorming.

A third purpose of brainstorming is that it forces people to approach a problem in different ways. Several years ago I came across a little exercise that I like to use to encourage people to think in new ways. Look at the circle below. Draw four straight lines through the circle to divide it into as many pieces as possible.

Many people draw four lines through the middle like they were cutting a pie. However, you can only get eight pieces that way. But no one said the pieces had to be equal in size. If the lines do not meet in the center, you can get up to eleven different pieces.

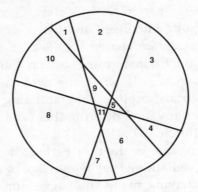

Brainstorming helps you to think outside the lines, to create new ideas.

A fourth purpose of brainstorming is that it allows you to cover a lot of ideas in a short time. Not every idea is worth taking the time of the whole group to discuss. If someone suggests an idea that does not merit the group's spending time on it, it can be passed over when the evaluation period comes. However, if you discussed the merits of each idea at the time the ideas were suggested, then you would have to deal with each idea individually.

How to Use Brainstorming

Brainstorming is not a teaching method that can be used by itself. It must always be used with other methods. Several of the teaching methods that have a high discovery quotient work well with brainstorming. Case studies, role play, questions, discussion, and even lecture combine well with brainstorming.

The rules for using brainstorming are simple:
1. Present the problem.
2. Ask for responses.

3. Record the responses.
4. Evaluate the responses.

To use brainstorming, first you must present a problem situation. Then ask your members to suggest solutions to the problem. You may present the problem in the way you think will work best. However you present the problem is fine—just as long as the people understand what the problem is. A good way to present a problem situation is to use a role play that covers the problem you are trying to find solutions to. Other ways of presenting the problem would be to read a case study or present a brief lecture in which you state the problem.

After you have presented the problem, it is time for members to respond. This is, of course, the heart of brainstorming. If you have not used brainstorming, tell your members what you want them to do. Be sure you tell them that at this point they cannot evaluate or comment on suggestions members make. This step will come later. Right now, encourage them to think outside the lines and suggest any idea that comes to their mind that is remotely related to the topic. It does not make any difference whether an idea is good or bad. A bad idea may trigger a good idea in someone else.

Once you have presented the problem, then you need to have some method of recording group members' responses. You can use a chalkboard, overhead cel, or large sheet of paper. If you do not have access to any of these, you can ask a person to write down the ideas on a sheet of notebook paper. However, if the group can see the ideas suggested they will be less likely to suggest something that has already been recorded. I like to use a large sheet of paper; I can keep the ideas to refer to later. If you use a chalkboard, you can ask someone to copy the ideas for you, so you will have a copy.

The final step is to evaluate the responses. Depending on the amount of time you have available, you can either evaluate the responses in this session or at a later one. Most of the time, you will evaluate the responses in the same session. Unless you are involved in a major project of some type, you probably will use brainstorming as a part of a lesson plan. If you do that, you will want to evaluate the groups' ideas as an immediate follow-up to the brainstorming session.

Let me mention a slight variation of brainstorming which Jerry Richards of Franklin, Tennessee, shared with me. Instead of brainstorming, use brainwriting. It involves the same ideas as brainstorming except you ask people to write their ideas on a sheet of paper.

Use a sheet of regular typing paper. Section it off by drawing lines on it to make it resemble a tictac-toe game. Then pass this sheet around to the whole group and ask each person to write an idea in one of the boxes without reading the other ideas. You could give group members a sheet of paper and ask them to write in as many different ideas as they can think of.

This variation has the advantage of getting people's ideas without their hearing the comments of others. Sometimes people will get into a certain frame of mind when the first person makes a suggestion. Of course, the opposite is true also. At times people's minds are stimulated by what others have said. However, brainwriting is worth trying.

Advantages and Disadvantages of Brainstorming

Brainstorming has several advantages. It introduces new ideas. It lets people participate in the class discussion and get their word in. It encourages the normally quiet person to speak up. It lets the group discover the ideas, so they feel they have had a part in the process.

Brainstorming has some disadvantages. If members do not grasp fully the problem you are trying to solve, their suggestions may not be helpful. The members may not have the knowledge background to make creative suggestions. These disadvantages can be overcome by presenting the problem clearly and by being certain that they have the background to make intelligent responses.

How to Use Brainstorming with Other Teaching Methods

Brainstorming is not a method that can stand alone. It must be used with other methods. The problem must be stated. Ideas must be evaluated and priorities must be assigned to them. Just suggesting a lot of ideas is of little value. If you do not go through the whole process, then you have wasted your class members' time.

How many different methods can brainstorming be used with? Brainstorming can be used as a companion method to the other four basic methods.

Lecture and Brainstorming

Brainstorming works well with lecture. Let's use an example.

Passage to be studied: Luke 11:1-13

Teaching Aim: To identify Jesus' instructions on prayer, and to choose one way members can improve their prayer life

After a lecture on the biblical passage, ask members to brainstorm ways Christians can improve their prayer life. By using brainstorming as a part of the application process, members can take advantage of the information shared in the lecture. Talking about what they have just heard will help them to remember the points of the lecture.

When they have made their suggestions, ask them to choose one of the suggestions that they will work on to improve their own prayer life. To help them make this commitment, use a personal commitment form:

PERSONAL COMMITMENT FORM

Because I want to grow in my prayer life, I commit myself to the following for four weeks:

_____

_____

_____   _____
    (name)   (date)

Members can keep this form in their Bible as a way to
help them follow through on their commitment.

Here you have combined brainstorming with lecture to
keep the class session from being all telling or lecture. You
have used brainstorming to help members discover how
the principles of God's Word apply to their personal
prayer life.

Case Studies and Brainstorming

Brainstorming also works well with case studies. You
could use the following case study to begin a lesson on
integrity. Bill Godfrey lived in a community in which
most of the people belonged to X religion. In the past a lot
of tension had existed between members of that religion
and nonmembers. In recent years these tensions had
eased, and Bill had been elected to a position on the city
council. This was the first time anyone could remember
that a person who was not a member of X church had
been elected to a city-wide position. Shortly after he was
elected, Bill received a copy of a letter sent by the council
chairman to a trucking business near Bill's house. The letter showed that the city council had paid this trucking
business $10,000 for "services rendered." Since the ad-
dress of the trucking business was near Bill's home, he
tried to locate it but could not. Instead, he found that the
address to which the check was sent was an X church. The
head of the supposed trucking firm was the head of the
church. When Bill asked the council chairman about the

letter, the chairman told him that he should not have received a copy of the letter. It was a just a mistake, and Bill should just forget that he had seen it.

After reading this case study, let members brainstorm what Bill's options were.

Role Play and Brainstorming

Role play can be combined with brainstorming equally well. To conclude a lesson on ministry, have two people act out the following role play. Brenda's husband had just died. Alice, whose husband had been dead for about a year, came to see her. Alice's conversation went something like this: "Brenda, I know just how you feel. I know it is going to be hard on you. It is so hard on me. I just hate to go to bed at night. I stay up late until I am sure I'll fall asleep. It is so hard. I miss my Paul so much, but it is God's will, and we mustn't question God."

Let members suggest all the things Alice did wrong in her visit to Brenda. Then distribute brainwriting forms and let members suggest all the things Alice could have done right. When members have finished writing, ask them to share what they have written. Ask them to brainstorm any additional ideas they may have.

After they have made their suggestions, ask them to choose the top five suggestions they should do to minister at the time of death and the top five things they should avoid doing or saying at the time of death.

Questions and Brainstorming

Questions and brainstorming are quite closely linked. After you have presented the problem situation, you must ask what the class is to decide. Be sure your questions ask exactly what you want. Members must understand what you want. Be specific. The type of questions you ask will determine the success of the brainstorming. Keep the questions related to the scriptural background as much as

possible. In the above lesson on prayer, ask members to
suggest specific ways they can improve their prayer life.

How Does Brainstorming Encourage
Discovery Learning?

Brainstorming has a high discovery quotient. Let's do a
little brainwriting now. Instead of my *telling* you how well
brainstorming relates to discovery learning, how about
making that decision yourself. First, prepare a brainwriting graph. Now, look back over this chapter and write the
ways that brainstorming can encourage discovery
learning.

7
Role Play in the Classroom

"Never criticize others until you walk in their shoes." My mother often repeated that sage advice. How do you walk in someone else's shoes?

Role play offers the opportunity to slip into shoes that do not belong to you, so you can feel what it's like to experience what other people are going through.

An example of the ultimate role play is *Black Like Me*, a book by John Howard Griffin. Griffin underwent a series of medical treatments to change the color of his skin temporarily. He then passed himself off as a black man and traveled through the state of Mississippi. His was as near a complete role play as is possible.

What I have in mind for your Sunday School class is a little less drastic than that. However, role play is a powerful teaching method for making application of the Scriptures. It ranks right at the top of the discovery quotient.

Role Play Defined

Role play is the process by which persons act out what other persons would feel, do, or say. The persons doing the role play are given only the general setting of the event. They must decide what to say or how to act. Often the event involves a conflict, and, in contrast to a biblical skit or biblical simulation, role play is set in the present. Having to put biblical ideas into present-day terminology and setting is one of the strong points of role play.

The Purpose of Role Play

Role play attempts to get people to feel—to discover —what is going on in someone else's life. What does it feel like to be a member of a minority race? What does it feel like to be the only senior high student in your group who does not use drugs?

I had the privilege once of preaching in a Korean church. My family and I were the only Anglos present. All the service was in Korean. The only thing I understood in the service were the words *Jim Taulman* when the pastor introduced me. I don't know how much anyone else got out of the service, but I learned just a little bit about what it means to be a minority.

Role playing helps your members get inside someone else's feelings. Of course, one can never understand exactly how someone else feels. Even though I was in the minority in the Korean church, when the service was over I knew I would once again be a member of the majority. However, the experience did give me a glimpse into how others must feel.

Role play can also be used to teach or show how to do some function. When I was a Junior boy in the Easton Heights Baptist Church in Tulsa, we often used role play. (I doubt if anyone in the church called it role play, but that's what it was.) The only situation I remember being acted out dealt with a Christian calling on a non-Christian and leading the person to Christ. As I remember, the Christian always won. In that sense, the role play was not accurate. When I tried to lead someone to Christ in real life, it wasn't always as easy as the role play had suggested. Role play can be used to set up a mock experience and let members share how they would respond. My earlier experience would suggest that the role play be honest and true to life. If it isn't, it is of little value.

How to Use Role Play

Role Play, like other teaching methods, has certain steps that need to be followed if it is to be as effective as it can be. Let me suggest seven steps you need to follow in preparing to present a role play.[1]

Determine Your Direction

As with all teaching methods, you need to know where you are going. The Teaching Aim shapes the role play—not the other way around.

Role play is not just letting people act out something. You need to have a goal or purpose in mind. That purpose or aim will determine how you set the boundaries for the role play itself. For each role play, you need to ask: What do I want to accomplish?

Let's pick an example and follow it through these seven steps. Let's assume you teach a coed class of young adults. The lesson title for this coming Sunday is " Ministering in the Name of Jesus." The text is Acts 6:1-6. The Teaching Aim you have set for your class is: to lead members to understand how the early church ministered to those in need, and to discover ways our class can minister to those who have lost their spouse.

With these givens, a role play would be an excellent way to create interest or to make application. Let's use it as a way to create interest, although you could use it as a way to apply the lesson as well.

Your task is to present a role play that will help your class discover how to minister to those who have lost their spouse.

Establish the Setting

If you are going to present a role play that will accomplish that Teaching Aim, you will have to structure the setting so it does that. You will need to set up a ministry opportunity from which members can learn how to minister (or how not to minister).

The role play needs to have enough design to it so the members can understand the problem. In the role play we are developing, several aspects should be present: (1) a situation in which a woman (or man) has lost her husband (or wife); (2) a situation in which some physical, emotional, or spiritual need exists; (3) the need must be such that a Sunday School class can meet it.

With these requirements let's set the stage for the case study by using the following: Cheryl's husband, Roy, was only twenty-eight years old when he was killed by a drunken driver. Roy had not been wearing his seat belt when he was thrown from the car and killed as a drunken driver ran a stop sign and broadsided Roy's car. Cheryl and Roy had only recently moved to the community. They did not have any family within several hundred miles. Cheryl was a dentist and had just opened a practice. The couple had no children.

With this information, you could go in several different directions. If this were a safety meeting, you could develop a role play that revolved around the need to wear seat belts. If this were a temperance lesson, you could develop a role play around what the class could do to get drunken drivers off the street.

However valid these two approaches may be, neither fits into the Teaching Aim which we have chosen. The aim shapes the design of the role play. Since your aim is to discover how the class can minister to people who have recently lost their spouses, that is the direction you must go.

After setting up the event, add the following instructions for those who will do the role play: your purpose is to role play what could be done to help Cheryl in the days following Roy's death and the week following the funeral.

Those instructions limit the direction the role play can take and keep the participants from going off in a direction you do not want to go.

Enlist the Participants

You need to enlist as many people as you need to accomplish the role play. I have found it best to develop role plays that call for two or three people. More than that creates a lot of dynamics, and it becomes harder to keep on the aim. For our role play, let's enlist two members of the Sunday School class to play Judy and Jim, and someone to play the part of Cheryl. Give them the following instructions: you are to visit Cheryl in her home the day before the funeral to minister to her in behalf of the Sunday School class. You may want to have a follow-up visit a week later.

In selecting participants, be careful that you do not select someone who would find it difficult to do the role play. If you have someone in your group who has recently lost a spouse, I would not use that person in a role play of this type. A group I led at a conference center once chose a recent widow in order to add reality to the role play. The woman was far enough along in her grief process that she could handle the stress.

How far in advance should you enlist the participants? If you have never used role play, you might call the people a day or so in advance and ask them to help you. However, I have found that it works well to enlist participants on the spot and ask them to participate without a lot of advance notice. They may need a few minutes to determine who will play what role and how they will go about doing it. The participants might go outside the classroom while you prepare the class.

Prepare the Audience

Before the role play begins, prepare the audience. Divide the class into two listening teams. Ask one team to look for all the things the two visitors did right. Ask the other to look for all the things they did wrong.

Another possibility would be to give each member a listening guide like the following:

Role Play Listening Guide

1. What were the circumstances in the role play?
2. How many people were involved?
3. What was the aim of the role play?
4. Did the role play accomplish the aim? Why or why not?
5. What have you learned as a result of this role play?

As group members listen, they can make notes so they can discuss the role play when it is over. This listening guide has the advantage of making participants out of all the class. The class members are not just observers; they are a part of the role play.

Present the Role Play

When the audience has been prepared and the participants are ready, ask the participants to present the role play. Avoid using props unless they are essential to get the message across.

Although a role play differs from a skit in that the participants make up their own dialogue, let me create a dialogue for our purposes. (You can also use this dialogue as a case study on ministering.)

Jim: It looks like she is home. Her car is in the garage.

Judy: It doesn't look like anyone else is here. I'm glad we came. (rings door bell)

Judy: Hi, Cheryl. We wanted you to know that your Sunday School class is supporting you and praying for you during this time.

Jim: We are sorry about Roy's death. I'm sure it must be very difficult. We just want you to know if there is anything we can do to help you, all you have to do is let us know.

Cheryl: Hi, Judy and Jim. Come on in. I just finished talking to my parents. They are trying to get a flight out in the morning. Yes, it is very difficult. (breaks down and cries)

Jim: Now, Cheryl, you mustn't cry. I know just how you feel. My aunt died last year, and I still miss her.

Cheryl: I just don't see why God did this to me and Roy. We were just getting started in life. We had both been in school for so long, and we were just getting to the point where we could start a family. We had just bought this new house. I just don't see why God took him.

Jim: Now, Cheryl, we mustn't question God. The Bible says that all things work together for good.

Cheryl: I don't believe that. How can this be good?

Judy: I read that verse the other day in a modern translation, and it gave me a new insight. It said that God works in all things for good. I see that to be quite a different meaning. I do believe that God can work in this and bring some good out of it.

Jim: Well, we didn't come here to talk theology. We came to try to help. We just want you to know that if there is anything we can do to help, you just let us know.

Cheryl: Thanks, Jim, but I can't think of a thing.

Judy: Cheryl, I know your family doesn't live here, and until they arrive, we want our Sunday School class to be your family. Some of the women have prepared food for you and your family when they get here.

Cheryl: That would be appreciated. I am so upset that I haven't even thought about preparing food.

Judy: Tomorrow is Jim's day off. You said that your parents would be flying in. I'm sure Jim would be glad to meet them for you.

Cheryl: Well, I do need to get to the beauty parlor in the morning. I had just told Dad and Mom to take a cab from the airport. I hate to put you out.

Jim: No bother. I'll be glad to do that. Just let me know their flight number. I told you if there was anything we could do . . .

Judy: I wonder, too, Cheryl, if you have enough room for everyone to stay? We have plenty of room at our house. Sue Wilson also volunteered her house as well.

Cheryl: I think we have plenty of room. I'm not sure my brother is going to be able to get here. He is in the navy, and I'm not sure whether he is going to get to come. Dad is working on that. I'll have room for Roy's parents and my parents, but I may need a place for my brother.

Judy: I want to pass on an offer from Bill and Sandra Underwood. I know you do not know them well, but they have offered to house sit during the funeral if you would like for them to do so. This might be a precaution you should take.

Cheryl: How thoughtful! I appreciate that. We have had some break-ins nearby, and I would feel a lot better if someone were here. You all have thought of everything.

Jim: Well, as I said, if there is anything we can do, you just let us know.

Cheryl: Well, I can't think of anything, Jim. You all have been very kind.

Judy: Cheryl, I know that your parents will have some

errands to run when they get here. We have the extra
car, and if they need it, it is available.

Cheryl: That would be appreciated. Mother wanted to get
her hair done, too, and I was not able to get her an
appointment at the same time I made mine. So the car
might be helpful. I'll let you know.

Judy: We need to be going now. I'm sure you have several
things you need to do. Jim, why don't you lead us in
prayer.

Jim: Father, we pray for Cheryl in this time of her loss. We
ask you to comfort her. Help her not to question You
but to accept Your will for her life. In Jesus' name.
Amen.

Cheryl: Thank you for coming.

Judy: Someone will be by with some food in the morning.
We have meals planned for the next several days. I'll
call in the morning to find out what time your parents are arriving. I'll be praying for you through out
these next several days.

Jim: As I said, just let us know how we can help.

Cheryl: Thanks, Jim, you all have helped a great deal. I
can't think of anything else. Thanks for coming. I appreciate it so much. Thank all the Sunday School
class for me.

Analyze the Role Play

After the role play, the next step is to analyze what
happened. Let's assume that you assigned the two listening teams to discover what the visitors did right and what
they did wrong.

The team that is to look for what the visitors did wrong
has several things to report. I would mention at least the
following points: (1) Don't ask what you can do. (2) Never tell someone not to cry. (3) Do not tell people that you
know how they feel because you don't. (4) Don't grieve
over your own loss. (5) Don't defend God. (6) Don't quote

Scripture without having some idea of what it means. (7) Cheryl may have needed to talk about theology—at least she should have been offered an opportunity to raise questions about God if she so desired. (8) Don't use prayer to make your point in an argument.

Although the group did some things wrong, they also did several things right that the other listening group could report. (1) They went immediately to the house. (2) They expressed their grief. (3) They used the word *death* as a way of helping Cheryl accept what had happened to her. (4) Judy made several specific offers of help instead of asking what they could do. (5) They did pray—although it was not the kind of prayer they should have prayed.

You may see other things the two did right or wrong. The advantage of using listening teams is that one person will catch something someone else will miss.

Evaluate the Role Play

The final step in the role play is to evaluate it and draw conclusions from it. Based on the information we have here, I would suggest at least the following conclusions could be drawn. (1) At the time of grief, people do not think clearly. Make specific suggestions about what you will do. (2) The class needs to set up some kind of system whereby it can provide for food in event of a funeral. (3) Ministry in time of grief should be more than a one-time event. (4) Ministry at time of death is needed.

Advantages and Disadvantages of Role Playing

Role play ranks high in discovery learning. Few other teaching methods rank as high as role play does in helping people discover things for themselves. Role play helps people analyze situations and discover answers for themselves. It does not deal with just factual knowledge; it deals with the levels of learning beyond recall and comprehension. Role play helps members apply the Scripture, analyze its meaning, pull meaning from the Scripture, and evaluate what it means for their lives.

Role play helps you translate the Bible into today. For example, how would you do a role play of the dishonest steward (Luke 16:1-13)? Or how about role playing a modern-day experience of Jesus' family coming to take Him home (Mark 3:20-21,31-35)?

Role play lets you put into practice what you believe. It lets you react with others who believe differently. It lets you see how others would respond in similar circumstances. It lets you demonstrate how something can be done and analyze what wasn't successful.

However, role play does have some disadvantages. Role play takes time to develop. It is not something that is put together quickly without thought and planning. You are dependent upon the members of the class to participate. If they are unable—or unwilling—to participate, you must use another method. Role play can expose a lot of feelings. A teacher or class unable to handle the expression of feelings can feel uncomfortable if members express too much emotion.

However, the advantages of role play far outweigh the disadvantages. Role play can be an exciting method of helping people discover biblical truths for themselves.

How to Use Role Play with Other Teaching Methods

Role play—as is true with most other teaching methods—cannot stand on its own. It must be combined with other teaching methods.

Questions are an integral part of role play. A role play is incomplete without the analysis of the circumstances. Teachers who would get the most out of role play will develop perceptive questions to ask when the role play is over. They will use the questions to draw out the meaning of the experience and the application it has for today.

Group discussion also is involved directly in role play. Members can discuss what the role play meant to them.

Brainstorming can also be used to evaluate the role-play experience. You could brainstorm ministries Judy and Jim could have offered to Cheryl. In so doing, you would compile a list of ministries that could help members and prospects for your Sunday School class.

Lecture can also be combined with role play. After a short lecture on Acts 6:1-6, you could call on some of the group to role play a modern experience in which the church ministered to someone who had lost his or her spouse.

Case studies are easily translated into role-play situations. Instead of reading a case study, enlist class members to role play it.

Role play works well with nearly every other teaching method. It is a skillful way to understand what God's Word means today.

How Does Role Play Help in Discovery Learning?

Tremendously! Role play has a high discovery quotient. It works well as a means of showing, not telling. A youth who would act out how it feels to have your best friend betray you can grasp some of the loneliness Jesus felt when all the disciples left Him. A woman who would role play asking that her two sons might be given positions of honor in a new company could understand better the feelings of James and John's mother when she asked that favor for her sons (Matt. 20:20-28). Role play ranks high in discovery learning.

Examples of Role Play Situations

The following situations could be used as a basis for role-play experiences. Each of these situations is a modern-day example at least loosely tied to a particular Scripture.

Scripture: Matthew 18:21-35

Characters: 3
Setting: First scene. An owner of an investment firm discovers an employee has been getting insider information and making millions of dollars for himself through his own investments. He starts to blow the whistle on the employee and go to the government with the information. The employee begs for his job and the owner relents.

Second scene. The forgiven employee returns to catch the housekeeper stealing some stamps out of his desk. The housekeeper pleads for forgiveness and asks to keep the needed job. Instead, he immediately fires the housekeeper for dishonesty.
Scripture: Matthew 13:44-45
Characters: 2
Setting: Two businessmen (or women) are talking. One of them offers the other an opportunity to invest in a good deal. However, the amount of money required is more than the other has. In order to get the money, he mortgages his house and car.
Scripture: Genesis 30:25-43
Characters: 2
Setting: Two characters are talking. One of them tells the other that he overheard the owner of a small clothing manufacturer for which they work telling a business associate that he had put one over on his employees. He had been able to arrange the books so that it looked like the company had experienced a sizable loss during the past several years, and they had forced the union to make some benefit concessions during the last contract negotiations. The other employee says that is all right because he and one of the inspectors have been marking as rejects clothing that was perfectly good and selling it to some of the company's customers at a much lower cost than it normally sold for, and the two employees have been pocketing the profit.
Scripture: Matthew 26:69-75; Mark 14:66-72; Luke 22:56-

62; John 18:15-18,25-27
Characters: 4
Setting: Four people are sitting around a table in a coffee
shop drinking coffee and talking. One of them is a Christian. Each of the other three says something to the Christian about going to church or being a church member or a
Christian. Each time the Christian denies being a Christian. The last time the Christian is asked, he starts to tell a
dirty joke to prove he is "one of the boys."
Scripture: Matthew 26:6-13; Mark 14:3-9; John 12:1-8
Characters: 2
Setting: Two church members are talking about a third
member who recently had given a rather sizable inheri-
tance she had received to a foreign missions offering. One
of them criticizes their fellow church member strongly for
doing this because she should have used the money to
take care of her aging mother.
Scripture: John 13:1-17
Characters: 3
Setting: Two church members were talking about the
poor janitorial service the church has. They specifically
comment on how dirty one of the rest rooms is because
someone had vomited all over the floor and not cleaned
up the mess. As they talk, the pastor comes in as though
he is in a hurry. They want to talk to him about the problem, but he says he doesn't have time now. He has to clean
up the rest room.

8
Thinking Like
a Biblical Character

What did Judas feel like the night he betrayed Christ? What did Job feel like when he encountered God? What did Paul feel like in prison?

These questions are important to a study of the Bible. In one sense these questions cannot be answered. In another sense, they *must* be answered.

Biblical Skits Defined

Biblical skits will help people find an answer that cannot be discovered in any other way. A biblical skit is a brief exchange between two or more biblical characters. These characters can be real or imaginary. They can be persons mentioned in the Bible, or they can be characters you have created to share their feelings about events in the Bible records. We do this every Christmas with the innkeeper. Although we often refer to the innkeeper, the Bible does not even mention such a person. However, we assume that because there was an inn, there also was an innkeeper.

The Purpose of Biblical Skits

Biblical skits provide Bible teachers with a method of teaching that will enable them to use their creative abilities to present biblical events and personalities to their classes. Biblical skits have the unique ability of letting the writers of the skits superimpose their understanding or grasp on a particular personality or event. This is both an advantage and a disadvantage.

It is an advantage because you can communicate feelings and insights that will make the biblical characters and events come alive. It is a disadvantage because you must be certain that the feelings and insights you ascribe to the biblical characters are accurate. This does not mean that you cannot put some modern-day words and expressions in the mouths of the biblical characters. Just be certain that whatever you place in the mouths of biblical characters does not distort or alter the character. Let me illustrate what I mean.

In the skit, "Guess What? We're Moving" I have placed some modern-day expressions and feelings in Sarah's mouth. Although we do not have a record of what she said when Abraham came home and told her they were leaving, I think we can be certain that what I have written wasn't what Sarah said. However, surely somewhere in the process, Sarah felt like Abraham was foolish for leaving Haran and not even knowing where he was going.

What I have tried to do is to present the struggle in modern terms to capture the feelings of people today who are asked to follow someone else's commitment to God without having God speak directly to them. My hope is that the skit will help people studying the life of Abraham and Sarah to understand the tension and struggle they went through as Abraham pulled up roots and went out "without knowing where he was going" (Heb. 11:8, GNB).

I hope that I have not given a distorted picture of Abraham and Sarah. In my own mind I picture Abraham struggling with this call—much like some today struggle with the call to preach. I don't think that God spoke to him out of the blue, and Abraham just went home and packed his tent and left. Following God is a serious pilgrimage. It is not something that should be undertaken lightly. Abraham did not take it lightly, nor should we.

Biblical skits can be used to challenge people today with the eternal message of God's Word. The skits give you an opportunity to couch the characters in today's language, so your class members can identify more easily with them. In that way, they can understand that the message of the Bible applies to their lives today—not just to the characters in the Bible.

How to Construct Biblical Skits[1]

Constructing biblical skits is more difficult than any of the previously discussed teaching methods. However, it is also an exciting teaching method.

You can have several different styles of biblical skits. You can use only Scripture verses ("The Earth Is the Lord's"). Choose a passage that lends itself to several voices. Divide the passage into different speaking parts. Try to let the number of voices come naturally from the text.

You can use Scripture but intersperse it with a modern comment or application. "Lovest Thou Me, More Than These?" in chapter 3 is an example of this type.

You can use biblical skits to report on biblical events. "Whoever Thought It Could Happen in Israel?" is an example of this type of skit.

A fourth type of biblical skit uses the biblical event as its basis. However, it does not attempt to report accurately on the event, but uses the event as a way of applying biblical truth to modern needs. "Guess What? We're Moving!" is an example of this type of skit.

How to Use Biblical Skits

Biblical skits can be used in various ways in the classroom. You can use biblical skits to create interest. If you have a departmental period in which you meet with other classes, you can use a biblical skit to create interest. You can also use it the same way in your individual class.

You can also use biblical skits to acquaint members with the biblical passage. Biblical skits provide a great way to survey a passage of Scripture. If you are studying a psalm, you can use a skit that contains only the Scripture or intersperses the Scripture with a refrain or modern comment. You can also use a skit to summarize the content in a passage.

Biblical skits can also help you apply the Scripture to life. I used "Lovest Thou Me, More Than These?" in my Sunday School class as a part of the application when we were studying the twenty-first chapter of John.

You can use biblical skits in just about any phase of your lesson. It all depends on how you construct them and how you use them.

How to Use Biblical Skits with
Other Teaching Methods

Biblical skits work well when used with other teaching methods.

You can combine a biblical skit with a *lecture* to add variety and to create interest. If you have a lecture planned on some Old Testament event, write a biblical skit to summarize the event. Use this skit at the beginning to create interest in the event and to summarize the Scripture.

You can use a biblical skit at the conclusion of a lecture to apply the Scripture. Determine the main points of your lecture and then write them into a biblical skit.

You could also develop a biblical skit to present the Scripture itself if you are studying a passage like the Psalms that does not lend itself well to a narrative skit.

Biblical skits also work well with *group discussion*. You could use a skit to create interest, to study the Scripture, or to summarize the biblical text at the conclusion of the study and draw some application from it.

You can also use *questions* in biblical skits. "Lovest Thou Me, More Than These?" asks questions, and it is also a biblical skit. Using the skit ties the questions closely to the biblical event. The skit helps the listeners realize that Jesus is asking us the same questions He asked Simon Peter.

How Do Biblical Skits Help in Discovery Learning?

How do you think biblical skits work in discovery learning? If you have followed me up to this point, I'm sure you can answer this question as well as I. (But then, I'm not one to pass up another opportunity to encourage you to help your members discover Bible truths for themselves!) Biblical skits rank high in discovery learning. Biblical skits enable you as the teacher to point members in certain directions that you would like them to go. You can raise questions, you can plant ideas, and you can point out issues in the skits. Then you can switch to a modern application and help the members of your class to examine their own lives considering the questions, ideas, and issues raised in the skit. Instead of telling your members something, you are able to lead them to discover it for themselves. Biblical skits work well in discovery learning.

Examples of Biblical Skits

The following are some examples of various types of biblical skits.

WHOEVER THOUGHT IT WOULD HAPPEN IN ISRAEL?

Scripture: 2 Samuel 11:1—12:14
Voices: 2
Time: 2:30
   1: Whoever thought it would happen in Israel?

2: I just can't believe that King David would do such a thing!

1: That's what happens when kings begin to think they are more powerful than the people they serve.

2: It wouldn't have happened if David had gone to war that spring.

1: He wouldn't have been home to see Bathsheba bathing in the cool of the evening on top of the house.

2: Bathsheba should never have accepted his invitation to the palace.

1: I know that Uriah had been gone a long time, and things might not have been just right between them, but that's still no excuse for what she and David did.

2: David's scheme to hide his sin certainly backfired.

1: Even when he got Uriah drunk, Uriah would not go home to sleep with his wife. He said he couldn't do that while the rest of the army was on the battlefield.

2: What loyalty!

1: Uriah's loyalty to David and his country must have made David feel like a miserable traitor.

2: That is what makes the whole matter so ugly. Uriah was murdered just because he was faithful to the king. The king rewarded his loyalty by sentencing him to death.

1: Whoever thought it would happen in Israel?

2: It is still hard to believe.

1: But God has His ways of calling people to account for their sins.

2: Nathan certainly was courageous. David had already killed one man to hide his sin.

1: Nathan certainly slipped up on David's blind side.

2: He got David to condemn himself by telling that parable about the pet lamb.

1: I would have been afraid to point my finger at the king and say he was guilty.

2: But Nathan did it. He accused the king to his face.

1: And that was when David's greatness came through.
He confessed his sin, and God forgave him.

2: But David's home life would never again be the
same. His family had seen David's disregard for human life, and they copied his sin rather than his
confession.

1: What a tragedy that they saw the one and failed to
see the other.

2: God can forgive, but not even God can remove the
consequences of our sins.

1: Whoever thought it would happen in Israel?

2: I hope it never happens again anywhere else.

THE EARTH IS THE LORD'S

Scripture: Psalm 24
Voices: 2
Time: 1:30

1: The earth is the Lord's,

2: And the fullness thereof;

1: The world,

2: And they that dwell therein.

1: For he hath founded it upon the seas,

2: And established it upon the floods.

1: Who shall ascend into the hill of the Lord?

2: Or who shall stand in his holy place?

1: He that hath clean hands,

2: And a pure heart;

1: Who hath not lifted up his soul unto vanity,

All: Nor sworn deceitfully.

1: He shall receive the blessing from the Lord,

2: And righteousness from the God of his salvation.

1: This is the generation of them that seek him,

All: That seek thy face, O Jacob.

1: Lift up your heads,

2: O ye gates;

1: And be ye lift up,

2: Ye everlasting doors;
All: And the King of glory . . .
1: . . . the King of glory . . .
2: . . . the King of glory . . .
All: Shall come in.
1: Who is this King of glory?
2: The Lord strong,
1: . . . and mighty,
2: The Lord mighty in battle.
1: Lift up your heads,
2: O ye gates:
1: Even lift them up,
2: Ye everlasting doors;
All: And the King of glory . . .
1: . . . the King of glory . . .
2: . . . the King of glory . . .
All: Shall come in.
1: Who is this King of glory?
All: The Lord of hosts, he is the King of glory.

GUESS WHAT? WE'RE MOVING!

Scripture: Genesis 12:1-9
Voices: 2
Time: 3:45
Abraham: Sarah! Sarah!
Sarah: Yes, Abraham, what is it?
Abraham: I've got something to tell you.
Sarah: Well, go right ahead. I'm listening.
Abraham: I don't know exactly how to begin.
Sarah: How about at the beginning? That's always a good
    place to start something.
Abraham: But I'm not sure where the beginning of this is.
Sarah: What is it, Abraham? You're not going to try to tell
    me that you love me so much you're going to bring in
    another wife, are you?

Abraham: No, of course not. You know that even though others here in Haran do that, I don't believe it's right.

Sarah: What is it then? Are you going to divorce me?

Abraham: Sarah! How could you say such a thing? You know I could never do that.

Sarah: I wish you would tell me what it is. The suspense has to be worse than whatever you can say.

Abraham: (rapidly and almost under his breath) We're moving, and I don't know where we're moving to.

Sarah: What did you say? It sounded like you said we were moving, and you didn't know where we were moving to.

Abraham: That's exactly what I said.

Sarah: Are you sure you wouldn't just as soon take another wife? That sounds a whole lot less complicated. Most men when they have a mid-life crisis do something like bring home a new wife or buy a sporty new camel. But not you! You have to pick up and move. And you don't even know where you're going. Why can't you be like other men?

Abraham: Please, Sarah. Try to understand.

Sarah: I would like to, but I just can't understand why you would want to leave Haran. We have our new home here. I just bought the drapes for the living room. You just got all the landscaping done. I've just been elected president of the Haran Valley Garden Club. Now you say we are moving. Why do you want to leave?

Abraham: I don't want to leave.

Sarah: Now let me see if I have this straight. You come in here telling me that we are going to pick up and move from our new home and our friends, but that you don't want to do it? Then would you please tell me why we are moving?

Abraham: Because God told me to.

Sarah: This is even worse than I thought! It's bad enough

just to pick up and move away from all our family and friends, but now you say God told you to do it. Why can't my husband just have a normal mid-life crisis? When did God start talking to you? Are you sure it wasn't that lamb stew you had for lunch?

Abraham: No, Sarah. I've never been more sure of anything in my life. I don't want to move either. I like it here. But you know that we have talked about finding a better place to raise our children. You don't like all these pagan gods any more than I do.

Sarah: But do we have to move to some place that we don't even know?

Abraham: I'm certain that God wants us to leave. He said he would show us where we are to go as we follow Him. He promised to bless me and give me many descendants.

Sarah: Abraham, you have always been such a dreamer. Only you would even think of doing something like that. I guess that's why I love you so.

Abraham: Then you'll go with me? Even if I don't know where I'm going?

Sarah: Of course I will! I'd rather be with someone who is following God's will even though it may mean hardship and difficulties than to stay here in Haran with someone who refused to obey God's voice. Sure I'll go. But wouldn't you even consider a new sporty camel? I understand that Camel Caravan is having a sale this weekend.

9
You Were There

In our high school history class (Yes, they did have history then, just not quite as much of it!) our teacher would play records entitled "You Were There." The announcer reported events in history and interviewed people as though they were living in the midst of some particular event. It made history come alive, and I have always liked history since then.

Biblical Simulations Defined

We can do the same thing with the events in the Bible. The Bible is a history book. However, it is a history book of God's intervention in the lives of His people. That makes it the most exciting Book in the world.
Biblical simulations are an attempt to simulate or describe in modern terms what went on in the past. I like to use the same approach I heard in high school to present the events that took place in the Bible. Having a reporter interview people involved in a particular event offers the teacher many advantages. You can use any kind of framework or approach for the event as long as you are able to share what happened in the event with your members.

The Purpose of Biblical Simulations

Biblical simulations communicate biblical facts in an interesting and different way from other teaching methods. It is easy to read the Bible and miss some of the important facts. Biblical simulations enable you to group together facts and survey long passages of Scripture. By presenting the Scriptures in this manner, you are able to help your members more easily remember the facts of the Bible. The presentation of these facts becomes the basis for your lesson.

How to Construct Biblical Simulations

If you have ever had the opportunity of listening to someone teach or preach who was a great storyteller, you know how exciting the Bible can be. However, we often do not see the Bible as being exciting. Have you read anything exciting in 2 Kings lately? Yes, 2 Kings. Normally, we labor through 2 Kings when we read the Bible through, but that is about all the attention we pay to it. Second Kings can be exciting, but let me show you instead of telling you! Second Kings is full of pain, disappointment, death, tragedy, intrigue, victory, and defeat. This is the stuff from which good drama is made. An understanding of 2 Kings is also necessary to understand Jewish history.

Josiah's Reforms

Scripture: 2 Kings 22:1—23:35; 2 Chronicles 34:1—35:27
Voices: 4
Time: 7:00
Announcer: We interrupt our regular programming to bring you this special news bulletin. King Josiah is dead. I repeat: King Josiah is dead. He was killed this afternoon as he led Judah's army against the Egyptian forces led by Pharaoh Necho. The whole Judean army is in a rout. Right now it does not appear as though the Egyptian army is going to march on Jerusalem. However, we will keep you informed on the Egyptian army's every movement. In the meantime, I

have one of the king's armor bearers here. Benaiah, I
know this is a sad day for you, but would you tell our
audience how the king died?

Benaiah: King Josiah had heard that Pharaoh Necho was
on his way to meet the king of Assyria at Charchemish which is located on the Euphrates River. So
Josiah led the Judean army and went to Megiddo and
tried to stop him. In the midst of a hail of arrows,
some of the Egyptian arrows found their mark. He
wasn't killed immediately. Some of the servants and I
pulled him out of the battle and brought him immediately to Jerusalem. He died here.

Announcer: Why would the king fight the Egyptians?
They were not attacking Judah. As I understand it,
Pharaoh Necho tried to talk Josiah out of attacking.

Benaiah: No one will ever know, now that Josiah is dead.
Some of us think that Josiah was trying to get in the
good graces of the Babylonians. Necho was on his
way to join forces with the Assyrians to attack the
Babylonians. Josiah was attempting to stop him. If he
could have succeeded, he would have looked good in
the eyes of the Babylonians. Then they would have
been obligated to help him if Judah was ever
attacked.

Announcer: It is tragic that we have lost such a good king.
The future of the whole nation now lies in Egypt's
hands. Do you think they will attack Jerusalem?

Benaiah: At this point, I don't think so. Necho was in such
a rush to get to Charchemish. However, on his return,
I fully expect him to attack Jerusalem. We will have
about six to eight weeks to get ready before Pharaoh
Necho comes back this way.

Announcer: Thank you, Benaiah, for your account. We'll
let you get on with your business. I know this is a
perilous time for our nation. Our prayers are with
you and the others who are in positions of leadership.

Benaiah: Thank you. I must be getting back to the palace.

Announcer: If you have just tuned in, King Josiah is dead. He was wounded today at Megiddo and died here in Jerusalem. He will be missed. Josiah had charted a straight course for the nation. He enacted many reforms. Many have said that he was the greatest king since King David, nearly four hundred years ago. I'm standing in front of the Temple which had a special place in the life of Josiah. Hundreds of people have gathered here. They are just milling around. No one knows exactly what to do. Let me see if I can talk with some of the people who have gathered here. Pardon me, ma'am, I wonder if you would share your reaction to King Josiah's death?

Woman: My feelings can be summed up in one word: terrible. As you can see, I've been around a long time. I remember he was crowned king when he was only eight years old. After the evil reigns of Manasseh and Amon, Josiah was like a breath of fresh air. He repaired the Temple and got rid of those awful pagan shrines we had for so long. This is a sad day.

Announcer: Let me move over here to Shemaiah, one of the Levitical leaders. What about you, Sir? As a Levite, you have benefited rather directly from some of the king's reforms. What are your feelings about the king's death?

Shemaiah: I just can't believe he's dead. Only day before yesterday I saw him here in the Temple praying for guidance. He spent a lot of time here. You know, he was the one who restored the Temple and the worship of Yahweh, the true God.

Announcer: Some of our listeners may not be aware of all this. How could one man do such a gigantic feat?

Shemaiah: In the midst of the restoration of the Temple, Hilkiah, the high priest, discovered a copy of the Law of Moses. He gave it to Shaphan, the scribe, and when Shaphan read it to the king, the king took it quite seriously.

Announcer: What did he do?

Shemaiah: First he ordered the Temple leaders to ask the prophet. . . . Oh, I can't think of her name. I'll think of it in a minute. She was Shallum's wife. Anyway, the prophet issued a severe warning because the nation had not been obeying God's laws. However, she said —Huldah! That's her name! Huldah. I knew I'd remember it. Huldah said that because of Josiah's concern for the Law that God would grant the nation a reprieve. That's when all the reforms started.

Announcer: What kind of reforms did he bring about?

Shemaiah: I couldn't even begin to tell you all he did. He took all the objects used to worship Baal, the goddess Asherah, and the stars out to the Kidron Valley and burned them. I helped carry them out there. It was a time of rejoicing as the fire consumed those wicked objects.

Announcer: What else did he do?

Shemaiah: He removed all the pagan priests, the temple prostitutes, and tore down all the places where sacrifices were offered to the pagan gods. He even traveled all over the country himself to be certain that all evidences of pagan worship were destroyed. We went as far as Bethel tearing down pagan altars and killing the pagan priests.

Announcer: That seems rather severe.

Shemaiah: Yes, it was severe, but the survival of the nation was at stake. If we had not wiped out the pagan worship, the worship of these pagan gods would have destroyed us. It was either us or them.

Announcer: What was the reaction of the people to all this?

Shemaiah: Those who had vested interests in the pagan worship were strongly opposed, but many of the people supported the king in his reforms. They were especially supportive after the observance of the Passover.

Announcer: Tell us about that.

Shemaiah: Let me see. I think it was about seventeen—no, it was eighteen—years after Josiah came to power. All the pagan religions had been stamped out. Josiah not only eliminated the evil, but he put something positive in its place. That was when he commanded us to observe Passover. None of us had ever observed Passover. The scribes poured over the Law of Moses to discover how it should be done. The King himself donated animals out of the royal flock. Some of the leaders of the Levites contributed animals. I even contributed a few myself. I tell you, it was a glorious occasion. The Festival of Unleavened Bread lasted for seven days. I never thought I would get to see such an occasion. And that wasn't the last time we observed Passover. Josiah insisted that we obey the Law of Moses and observe it every year.

Announcer: Thank you, Shemaiah. You have helped us to remember some of the king's great achievements. These will go down in history, for he truly was a great king: one of Judah's greatest. Let's go back to the station now for a brief break. We'll keep bringing you updates on the situation as we learn them. This is a sad day in the life of Judah. King Josiah. Dead—at age 38. He will be missed. This is your roving reporter for station WJER in Jerusalem.

Did I help you to discover how you can use biblical simulations to lead your members to discover biblical truths for themselves? Could you use this biblical simulation to create interest in something that normally appears as uninteresting as 2 Kings? I should hope so. If you use biblical simulations, you will help your members discover truths about the Bible they did not know.

I did not include every fact the Bible mentions in these passages in 2 Kings and 2 Chronicles. I tried to include those that were most important. I think I have included the basic facts that you need to know about Josiah. All the details of Josiah's reforms were not included, but you can do this as you study the lesson.

How to Use Biblical Simulations

Let me walk you through the preparation and presentation of a biblical simulation. Let's assume the lesson is on Josiah. A week in advance, select the four people you want to serve as the four voices. At this point, you can use one of two approaches.

You can write out the simulation as I have done and give the written script to those who will participate. If you choose to do that, your preparation will consist in letting each participant become acquainted with the script. Using a script has the distinct advantage of including everything that you want included. It gives participants something solid to use. They may feel a little more secure. Writing the script will take a little more time initially, but less time in practice.

The second approach would be to present the simulation without the script. This method has the advantage of injecting more spontaneity into the simulation. It does take more time to rehearse and be sure that all understand what they are to say. The announcer or interviewer becomes most important. How the interviewer asks the questions will determine the success or failure of the simulation. Write out the questions you want the announcer to ask. Be sure that the interviewees know the answers. One danger to guard against if you do not use a script: be sure the participants do not inject something that is not true to the message of the Bible.

If you choose not to use a script, give instructions like the following to the participants.

Announcer

Scripture: Please study 2 Kings 22:1—23-35; 2 Chronicles 34:1—35:27 and familiarize yourself completely with the biblical material.

You are a reporter for station WJER in Jerusalem. You have just received word that King Josiah has been killed in battle. Interview the following three people in Jerusalem who are mingling in front of the Temple after they have learned of Josiah's death: (1) Benaiah, armor bearer for King Josiah who helped pull Josiah from the field of battle; (2) Woman (or man), who has lived through Josiah's reforms and is shocked at his death; and (3) Shemaiah, a Levite, who helped Josiah restore the Temple and eliminate paganism from the land. Read the descriptions of each of the following to determine the questions you will ask.

Benaiah

Scripture: Please study 2 Kings 22:1—23-35; 2 Chronicles 34:1—35:27 and familiarize yourself completely with the biblical material.

Tell how the king died, where the battle was, and why Josiah would even fight Pharaoh Necho when the Egyptians were not attacking Judah. Point out that Jerusalem is not in immediate danger, but that as soon as Necho returns from Charchemish, Necho will probably attack Jerusalem.

Woman (or Man)

Scripture: Please study 2 Kings 22:1—23-35; 2 Chronicles 34:1—35:27 and familiarize yourself completely with the biblical material.

Share that Josiah was crowned when he was eight, and he was completely different from Manasseh and Amon, his grandfather and father, who were nearly completely evil. Describe briefly Josiah's repair of the Temple and the removal of the pagan shrines.

Shemaiah

Scripture: Please study 2 Kings 22:1—23:35; 2 Chronicles 34:1—35:27 and familiarize yourself completely with the biblical material.

Relate how Josiah restored the worship of Yahweh through the efforts of Hilkiah and Shaphan. Describe Huldah's role. Point out how Josiah destroyed all the objects used to worship Baal, Asherah, and the stars, and burned them in the Kidron Valley.

Either approach will work well. Whichever approach you use, arrange a time to rehearse what you are doing.

One additional thought you might consider. As a companion to the simulation, develop a study guide for members to use. This will assure that they will pay attention to the simulation and pick up the facts that you want them to get.

If you have a departmental period you can join with several different classes who will be studying this same lesson. Present the simulation on Josiah to the whole group, and then present the specifics of the lesson in the individual classes. You can use the simulation as a springboard to a discussion.

How to Use Biblical Simulations with Other Teaching Methods

You can use biblical simulation as a complete teaching tool by itself. However, that is difficult to do. It takes a skill to write a simulation that would last the entire teaching period of thirty minutes or more. I did this once on Easter morning when I wanted to present the Easter lesson with a fresh twist. This simulation on Josiah only takes about seven minutes to present.

Because of this, you will need to use biblical simulations with other teaching methods. Simulations work well when used to:
- create interest,
- survey long passages of material,
- introduce a topic,
- discover what the Bible means.

Present the simulation and then combine it with another teaching method. Use the simulation on "Noah and the Flood" to create interest. Then present a brief lecture on the conditions that led up to the flood. Use a study guide or listening teams during the lecture, and then conclude by letting class members brainstorm what the message of Noah is for our day and time.

NOAH AND THE FLOOD [1]

Scripture Reference: Genesis 6:1—7:24
Voices: 5
Time: 8:00

Announcer: Good evening. This is eyewitness news from station WARK. This evening the news is rain! The country has never seen anything like this in our history. It has been raining steadily for days now, and serious flooding has already occurred in the low lands. Let's go to our weather reporter for an update on the weather.

Weather Reporter: Thank you. The conditions are serious. It has been raining steadily now for five days. All low-lying areas are under water. People who live along the river banks have moved out of their homes and headed for higher elevations. The wild animals and livestock are suffering tremendously. They are being swept away by the rapidly rising waters. There is no place where they can find safety. It doesn't look like any end is in sight for this rain. Our prediction is that the rain will continue for the foreseeable future.

In fact, our long-range forecast indicates that this storm will be around for a long time to come.

Announcer: Let me interrupt to ask a question. How widespread does this storm seem to be? Are we the only ones that are experiencing this terrible rain?

Weather Reporter: No, it is quite widespread. We have heard reports from Babylon and as far away as Damascus that it is raining there, too. It seems as if it is raining over the whole world.

Announcer: Can you explain what is happening? Where is all this water coming from?

Weather Reporter: Well . . . frankly, no. None of our knowledge about weather can explain what is happening. It's almost as if someone has opened windows in the sky and is pouring water out of them. We have had reports that water is even coming up out of the ground as well. If you want an explanation, you will have to look someplace else. I cannot explain it. All I know is that it is a serious event. Disaster is imminent.

Announcer: One of our reporters is standing by with a report which may shed some light on the situation. Eber, I understand that you have someone there who may be able to explain the situation.

Eber: Well, I have someone who has a suggestion about what is going on. I'm not sure anyone can explain it completely. I'm out at the edge of town and have a couple of people who have something interesting to share. Ma'am, I wonder if you would tell our audience what you told me earlier. What do you think is the cause of all this rain?

Wife: I'm convinced that this is all happening just like Noah said.

Eber: Excuse me, but some of our listeners may not know who Noah is and what he said. Would you tell them who he is?

Wife: He's that man who used to live in that house right there next to ours. Now he's in that big boat right over there. He's the one that we have been calling crazy for all these years. He's preached about some God of his going to send a flood. No one listened to him. Now I think he was right. Why didn't I listen to him?

Eber: Did anyone listen to him?

Wife: No one but his family. They just sort of went along with him, I think. After all, nothing like this had ever happened before.

Eber: You say his family listened? Tell us something about them?

Wife: Well, he had three children—all boys: Shem, Ham, and Japheth. Why, I saw those little boys grow up. I even sent wedding presents when they all got married. They had such lovely weddings, even if they didn't offer sacrifices to the gods.

Eber: Let me get this straight, now. On this big boat is Noah, his wife, his three sons, and their wives. That's eight people in all. Is that right?

Wife: Yes, and they have been in there for nearly two weeks now. They went in seven days before it started raining, and it's been raining for five days now.

Eber: Why did Noah say that his God was going to destroy this world?

Wife: He said that it was too evil. He said his God had created the world and that because it was so full of violence and wickedness, He was sorry He had created it. Now, since God had made it, He had a right to destroy it. He was going to destroy it with a flood and start all over again.

Eber: Thank you, Ma'am. Let me talk to your husband. Sir, you have a different opinion about all this. What is your view?

Husband: Well, I admit that the situation looks dark right

now. However, it'll stop raining. Always has. So, I expect some flooding, but the rain has to stop before long. There's not enough water to cover the whole earth like that man Noah said. Besides, there's no God powerful enough for that.

Eber: Can you tell us some more about this man Noah?

Husband: As far as I'm concerned, he's crazy. Senile. He's six hundred years old. Look at that big boat. It's still miles from the river. Even if the river does flood, it will never get up here.

Eber: Would you describe that boat for our listeners? You watched him build it, didn't you?

Husband: Sure did, and had a great many laughs along the way. Let's see now. It's about . . . 450 feet long, and I would say about 75 feet wide, and probably about 45-50 high.

Eber: How did they get inside? It doesn't look like there is any door.

Husband: There is one door: there on the side. You have to look carefully to see it. It is all sealed up. I watched them go in last week. After they went in, the door just closed up. I don't know how he closed it. It was almost as if an unseen hand reached down and closed the door after they all got inside. Can you imagine how silly all that looked. Here was a grown man and his grown sons and their wives getting into a boat out here in the middle of the desert. I can assure you we all had a good laugh as we watched them.

Eber: The boat looks quite sturdy. And it is big enough.

Husband: Not to be a seafaring man, I'd say he did a pretty good job of building it. He sealed it all with tar on the inside, so it wouldn't leak. It has three decks with a roof over the third deck. There's a space of about 18" right under the roof to let the smell out.

Eber: Smell? What do you mean?

Husband: Why, from all those animals! That crazy fool

took a pair of every kind of animals he could find. It
was a regular zoo around here for a while.

Eber: Why did he do that?

Wife: (interrupting) I'll tell you why! Because the world is
going to be destroyed by all this rain, that's why.
He's going to use those animals to start the world all
over again. We should have listened to him. He offered to let us go with him, but you said this could
never happen. Now look at all this rain. If I hadn't
listened to you, I wouldn't be here in all this rain. I'd
be inside that boat all safe and dry. But no. Mr.
Know-it-all isn't so smart now. Look at all that water
out there. I'm going to see if Noah will let me in the
boat. I should never have listened to you in the first
place.

Husband: Well, go right ahead. I'll be right here laughing
when the rain stops, and you come back out.

Eber: As you can hear, the weather conditions have begun
to take their toll on people's emotions. The water
continues to rise. It is getting deeper by the minute. It
is still several feet from the boat, but it certainly
looks like it is going to reach the boat soon. A crowd
has now gathered around this odd-looking boat.
Some of the people have begun to pound on the door,
yelling for Noah to open the door and let them in.
Women with babies in their arms are screaming and
crying, begging to be let in. But there is no sound
from inside. In fact, we have heard nothing from the
inside, nor have we seen any sign of activity from the
boat. The water is getting higher. It has now reached
the boat. The people around it are yelling and
screaming and clawing with their fingers trying to get
in. But there still is no sound from the boat. The water continues to rise. The boat has started to float
now. The people around it are screaming for help.
They're hanging on to pieces of boards and trees, still

trying to get inside. I'm not sure how much longer we'll be able to stay here. The water is rising rapidly. Any minute, now, it will get to our power source. When it does, we will be off the air, and then only the gods know what will happen to us. Until that time comes, I will try to keep you informed. It looks like Noah was right, after all. It looks like this might be the end . . . (at this point, cut the lights, leaving the room in darkness for a short time).

Advantages/Disadvantages

The biggest disadvantage to using biblical simulation is the time it requires to prepare it. It does not take any less time to let the group make their presentation without writing it all out. The group must have some time for rehearsal unless you have an exceptional class. You also need enough people in your class to present all the parts. However, I have used simulation to good advantage when every member of the class had a role to read. Just be sure you will have enough people present to read or present the simulation.

The advantages of using biblical simulation, however, far outweigh the disadvantages. Few teaching methods work as well in creating interest and surveying long passages of Scripture as does biblical simulation.

People will remember facts you include in a simulation far longer than if they just read them in the Bible. For example, how high was the window in Noah's ark? If you read the above simulation, I'm counting on you to remember that it was 18" inches high. I didn't remember that (although I had read the passage many times) until I wrote the simulation. If you did not remember that fact, how about some other fact that you did not know before you read the simulation?

How Do Biblical Simulations Help
in Discovery Learning?

Biblical simulations place the learners in the center of the experience. They participate in the event. They feel the emotions of the people. They place themselves in the role of the biblical characters. In short, they discover what it was like in biblical days.

Biblical simulations rank high in discovery learning. Few teaching methods can create interest, survey long passages of material, and introduce a topic as well as biblical simulations. The success of this method can be demonstrated quickly by using one of the two simulations with a group and giving them a pretest and posttest to see what they have retained. You have helped to create a situation that appeals to the eye and to the ear. Biblical simulations help people discover biblical truths for themselves.

Notes

CHAPTER 1

1. John R. Verduin, Jr., Harry G. Miller, Charles E. Greer, *Adults Teaching Adults* (Austin, TX.: Learning Concepts, 1977), 110.

CHAPTER 2

1. Leroy Ford, *Using the Lecture in Teaching and Training* (Nashville: Broadman Press, 1968), 7.

CHAPTER 3

1. Ralph G. Nichols and Leonard A. Stevens, *Are You Listening?* (New York: McGraw-Hill Book Company, Inc., 1957),34; cited in John W. Drakeford, *The Awesome Power of the Listening Ear* (Waco: Word Books, 1967), 26-27.

2. Mic Morrow, "Teaching Suggestions," *Bible Book Study for Adult Teachers* (Nashville: Baptist Sunday School Board, January-March), 101.

CHAPTER 4

1. Inman Johnson, *Of Parsons and Profs* (Nashville: Broadman Press, 1959), 78.

2. *Bible Book Study for Adult Teachers*, April-June, 1987, 28.

CHAPTER 5

1. Leroy Ford, *Using the Case Study* (Nashville: Broadman Press, 1969), 17.

2. *Nashville Banner*, 27 May 1987, A-1.

3. James E. Taulman, *Help! I Need an Idea* (Nashville: Broadman Press, 1987), 118. Read Genesis 39:1-23.

4. *Bible Book Study for Adult Teachers* (Nashville: Baptist Sunday School Board, April-June 1987), 162.

5. Taulman, *Help! I Need an Idea* (Nashville: Broadman Press, 1987), 117-118.

6. *Nashville Banner*, 30 May 1987, A-3.

7. Ibid., C-20.

8. Ibid.

CHAPTER 7

1. I am indebted to Thomas F. Staton, *How to Instruct Successfully* (McGraw-Hill Book Company, Inc.: New York, 1960), pp. 124-156 for his suggestion of the seven steps.

CHAPTER 8

1. For more information on how to construct biblical skits, see my *Help! I Need an Idea* (Nashville: Broadman Press, 1987), 21-55.

CHAPTER 9

1. *Bible Book Study for Adult Teachers: Resource Kit* (Nashville: Baptist Sunday School Board, October-December 1987). Used by permission.

Topical Index

Scripture Index